I0762629

PRAISE FOR

Jesus Will Meet You There

"In *Jesus Will Meet You There,* my friends Kristen Wetherell and Sarah Walton serve as wise and understanding guides through the all-too-common struggles we all have with loneliness, fear, doubt, and grief. They don't offer easy answers or trite formulas. Rather, they provide sound insight into who Jesus has shown himself to be and what he has shown he will do—to help us navigate our very real struggles in this world."

—NANCY GUTHRIE, author and bible teacher

"As we face difficulties, we tend to be far more focused on our own weaknesses, sins, and the painful struggles than we are on God's kind presence. Thankfully, Kristen Wetherell and Sarah Walton write out of the depths of their experiences, avoiding clichés while still gently reminding us that we are creatures with good limits who are deeply known and loved by our compassionate God. What we discover is that our God meets us in Christ and by his Spirit, offering us needed courage as we face the challenges of life."

—KELLY M. KAPIC, author of *You're Only Human*

"If you're struggling and want someone to walk with you, *Jesus Will Meet You There* is a must-read. Kristen Wetherell and Sarah Walton don't just offer wise biblical counsel; they vulnerably open their lives, sharing how Jesus met them in their pain and doubts and how he met people throughout the Gospels. You'll feel like you're sitting with two trusted friends over coffee."

—VANEETHA RENDALL RISNER, author of *Watching for the Morning*

"When life is challenging, we're tempted to retreat, but what a comfort to reach up for hope and be assured that Jesus will meet you there. This book provides accessible truths to the tender places that are bruised and broken by the Fall."

—KAREN HODGE, coordinator of Women's Ministry for the Presbyterian Church in America (PCA) and author of *Transformed* and *Life-giving Leadership*

"It's an inescapable truth: We are human. And if we're honest, we don't always welcome that reality. In *Jesus Will Meet You There,* Kristen Wetherell and Sarah Walton offer a deeply wise and refreshingly honest alternative to much of today's self-help literature. This book doesn't offer clichés or quick fixes. Instead, it bears witness to the lived, tested faith of two women who speak candidly about life's hardships, extend a steady hand to their readers, and gently lead them to Jesus."

—JONATHAN D. HOLMES, executive director of Fieldstone Counseling and interim executive director of CCEF

"In *Jesus Will Meet You There*, Kristen Wetherell and Sarah Walton offer weary believers a steady, Gospel-rich companion for seasons of suffering. They anchor readers in the good news of the incarnate Lord who embodied our weaknesses and who stands ready to help in time of need. Rather than promising instant relief, they patiently show us that when Jesus does not remove our thorns, he gives us something better: sufficient grace and power perfected in weakness. This book does more than explain suffering—it shepherds sufferers to the Savior."

—Eric Schumacher, author of *The Good Gift of Weakness: God's Strength Made Perfect in the Story of Redemption*

"In *Jesus Will Meet You There*, we learn to view our human weaknesses as opportunities for the light and strength of Christ to shine brightly in our lives. I saw my own struggles mirrored in every chapter of this book, but more importantly, I was encouraged to look to the Savior who carried my sins and my sorrows to his cross. No matter what shape weakness takes in your life, Jesus meets you there in faithfulness and love. This book is a comfort."

—Glenna Marshall, author of *Memorizing Scripture*, *Known & Loved*, and *Praying in Pain*

"George MacDonald once said, 'When God is about to make pre-eminent use of a person, He puts them in the fire.' *Jesus Will Meet You There* shows just how right he was. With personal stories and profound reflections on the character of God, Kristen Wetherell and Sarah Walton invite us to see that our suffering is never pointless and Jesus is never closer than when we are at our weakest."

—Aaron Armstrong, author of *Faith Simplified: What We Believe and Why We Believe It* and *I'm a Christian—Now What?: A Guide to Your New Life with Christ*

"*Jesus Will Meet You There* feels like a personal visit from Kristen Wetherell and Sarah Walton to comfort us in our suffering. It's as if these two friends have joined us on the couch—warm tea in one hand, the Scriptures in the other—to offer grace, truth, and soul-deep encouragement. They share vulnerably from their own valleys of pain and offer a sturdy, eternal hope for ours. Their relational warmth and theological depth make this a book I will eagerly give to any friend walking through hardship."

—Jen Oshman, author of *Very Good: What the Bible Says About Being a Woman*

Jesus Will Meet You There

Jesus Will Meet You There

FINDING STRENGTH AND COMFORT IN THE SAVIOR WHO UNDERSTANDS

Kristen Wetherell
and Sarah Walton

MULTNOMAH

Multnomah

An imprint of the Penguin Random House Christian Publishing Group, a division of Penguin Random House LLC

1745 Broadway, New York, NY 10019

waterbrookmultnomah.com

penguinrandomhouse.com

Italics in Scripture quotations reflect the authors' added emphasis.

Interior illustrations: Ievgeniia Lytvynovych/Getty Images, bird and flower art; Mirgunova/Adobe Stock, flourishes

LIBRARY OF CONGRESS CATALOGING-IN-PUBLICATION DATA

NAMES: Wetherell, Kristen author | Walton, Sarah, 1984- author
TITLE: Jesus will meet you there / Kristen Wetherell and Sarah Walton.
DESCRIPTION: First edition. | New York, NY : Multnomah, [2026] | Includes bibliographical references.
IDENTIFIERS: LCCN 2026010814 (print) | LCCN 2026010815 (ebook) | ISBN 9798217152315 hardcover | ISBN 9798217152322 ebook
SUBJECTS: LCSH: Christian life | Christian life--Biblical teaching
CLASSIFICATION: LCC BV4501.3 .W434 2006 (print) | LCC BV4501.3 (ebook)
LC record available at https://lccn.loc.gov/2026010814
LC ebook record available at https://lccn.loc.gov/2026010815

PRINTED IN THE UNITED STATES OF AMERICA

1st Printing

First Edition

The authorized representative in the EU for product safety and compliance is Penguin Random House Ireland, Morrison Chambers, 32 Nassau Street, Dublin D02 YH68, Ireland. https://eu-contact.penguin.ie

BOOKMAKING TEAM: Production editor: Jessica Choi • Managing editor: Julia Wallace • Production manager: Kevin Garcia • Copy editor: Kayla Fenstermaker • Proofreaders: Rachel Kirsch, Carrie Krause

Book design by Kim Henze Walker

For details on special quantity discounts for bulk purchases,
contact specialmarketscms@penguinrandomhouse.com.

To our loving Lord and Savior, Jesus.
Your nearness is our good (Psalm 73:28).

Contents

PART 4: PAIN

PART 5: DOUBT

PART 6: GRIEF

Introduction

Let's drop the facade for a moment, shall we? You know the one—where we all strive to convince ourselves (and one another) that we have it all together when, deep down, we're painfully aware we don't.

Underneath that veneer, we have far more in common than we realize.

We all long to be known and loved. Even more—to feel worthy of love. We exhaust ourselves trying to prove that we are, in fact, deserving of such adoration. So what do we do? We despise the weaknesses that reveal the cracks in our strength, we loathe the failures that eat away at our confidence, and we're afraid of being exposed for who we really are: limited and flawed humans.

But *why*? Why are we so ashamed to admit such an obvious, undeniable reality?

The answer is simple but hardly simplistic. It's *hard* to be human. Finite, imperfect, sinful human beings living in a world of unknowns, disappointments, pain, highs and lows, twists and turns. And that is far from easy.

We know this, but still we wonder, *Is it just me? Does anyone really understand the struggles inside me and the challenges coming at me from all sides?*

More importantly—*does God?*

Maybe you've heard the truth about Jesus or even walked faithfully with him for years, but still you wonder, *Is Jesus really present and invested in every aspect of my life?* The Christian answer, of course, is yes. But what does that look like in real life—in the trenches, past the clichés—in moments of desperation when God feels distant? If God cares for us but our circumstances don't change, what then? *Does Jesus personally draw near and empathize with me, even in the messy, undesirable, broken parts of my story?* These questions matter because we will trust God only to the extent that we believe he truly knows and loves us.

But if Jesus really does understand us and meet us in the seen and unseen places, the joyful and sorrowful ones, and the nitty-gritty corners of our humanity—this makes all the difference. We're here to tell you the answer is yes, Jesus is right beside you as one who's lived it himself. But first, we have to face reality.

FRAGILE AS DUST

We are as fragile and passing as dust (Genesis 3:19). We're here one moment, gone the next. We're painfully aware of this fact, but to our core, we despise it and desperately try to ignore it. We do everything we can to mask it. We try to control the uncontrollable, protect our stoic independence, and avoid anything that exposes our vulnerability.

Throughout our lives, we find ourselves in a race against time. We strive to leave our mark on this temporary world, abhorring our limitations and, underneath it all, longing for a place to belong. All the while, we work hard to distract ourselves from anything that might bear evidence to our fragility. But try as we might, the reality of our humanness confronts us around every corner.

This, in part, is what drew Kristen and me (Sarah) together ten years ago. After we connected through our church in the Chicagoland area, we discovered we were both struggling with chronic health issues, which eventually led to a diagnosis of Lyme disease for each of us. At the same time, I discovered that all my children carried the same disease, which I'd unknowingly passed on through gestation. As Kristen and I bonded over the limitations of our illness, along with countless other struggles—financial, special needs, and disability, to name a few—the Lord provided the opportunity to co-write our first book, *Hope When It Hurts: Biblical Reflections to Help You Grasp God's Purpose in Your Suffering*. It wasn't an easy endeavor with the challenges at hand, but our faithful God grew a passion within each of us to share how the hope of Jesus meets us in every aspect of life—especially in the difficulties.

Since those early days, the Lord has kept us dependent on him. I have since moved across the country, and Kristen has added kids to her family, and while much has changed, much has stayed the same. As we talked recently, we realized the Lord, once again, was placing on both our hearts a desire to grapple with our limitations. *What is God doing in our weakness and pain? Does faith mean trusting what I can understand or trusting God with what I can't?*

The need for this book became clear to us both as we continued to wrestle through our endless questions and the struggles of living in a human frame.

Can you relate? Ask yourself . . .

- Do I despise my failures, frustrated by all the ways I fall short?
- Am I weighed down by doubt, pain, grief, or loneliness?
- Do I wonder, *Does anyone really care about me?*
- Do I fear letting go of control?
- Am I always striving for the elusive promise of happiness in the world around me?
- Does my sense of worth ebb and flow with my performance and the opinions of others?

- Do I struggle to believe God cares about the details—the overwhelming to-do list, the strained relationship, or the day's disappointments?
- Am I frustrated by the limitations of my humanity?

Limitations are part of being human. They're what make us realize we're not the Creator. More importantly, every one of the above questions (and more) is meant to lead us to the One who is—to the God who draws near to the humanity we so often despise.

BETTER THAN YOU KNOW YOURSELF

What if our humanity isn't something to run from, though? Although we despise our weakness, what if being weak is the very thing that will lead us to experience a strength beyond our own? And what if being needy doesn't make us repulsive to God but actually tugs on his heartstrings? Maybe the things that we believe make us unlovable are, in fact, the very things that draw Jesus *toward* us in the first place.

Friend, if we stop striving to be something we're not, we'll find the Someone we most need. And in finding him, we'll find who we are meant to be. We'll discover that every fragile, beautifully complex part of us is *already* fully known and loved by God—the One who not only created us but also became like us.

And *that* is where our hope is found. In Jesus.

As we'll learn together in the pages ahead, God isn't a distant, uncaring God. His death and resurrection saved us, but his heart for us didn't end there. Jesus *became* like us in every way (other than sin), allowing him to now *sympathize* with us in every way.

He knows the frustrating limitations of your weakness.

He feels the torment of your fear and shame.

He bears the silent suffering of your loneliness.

He endures the weariness of relentless pain.

He gets the battle against doubt.

He suffers the agonies of profound grief.

Jesus knows us better than we know ourselves. And because he fully knows us, he is most able to care for us:

> As a father shows compassion to his children,
> so the LORD shows compassion to those who fear him.
> For he knows our frame;
> he remembers that we are dust. (Psalm 103:13–14)

HE WILL MEET YOU THERE

If we're honest, though, it doesn't always *feel* like God is near or compassionate, especially when life hits us square in the face or our prayers seem to go unanswered. Like us, maybe you've struggled to make sense of the pain God has allowed, and right now you're wondering if he's stored up his compassion for everyone but you.

It's okay to acknowledge your lingering questions, to remove the veneer of "acceptable Christianity." We won't be ready to trust God with everything if we haven't actually brought him everything, including the stuff that's confusing and messy. It's not until we're honest with ourselves, and with God, that we'll be ready to receive the truth: We have a Father who not only remembers our frame and feels compassion for us but also came to do something about it.

That hope is why this book has been written.

And it's what we'll explore in the chapters ahead as we journey through the New Testament, holding up a magnifying glass to the life of Jesus as he meets people just like us. We'll see how he experienced the depth of our humanity in his own body and how he was drawn personally and compassionately to the humanity of others.

Here you'll find short, accessible chapters, which can be read in the order they appear or in whatever order seems most applicable to you right now. You can read the book alone or walk through it with a friend or group, and you can personally apply each chapter by engaging with the reflection questions at the end. However you read it, our prayer is that you'll close this book with a renewed sense of Jesus's presence with you. And more than anything else, we pray that you'll have a greater understanding of who Jesus is and how personal he really is.

That he *really* knows you and that you can *really* know him.

We don't write from a place of theory; we write from the trenches of our daily realities. We're not here to offer you motivational fluff or false hope. We're here to walk alongside you, human to human, as we encounter the real, life-changing truth of who Jesus has shown himself to be in the Gospels. We're here to dwell on rock-solid, substantial truth that brings tangible hope and draws us near to the very heartbeat of God through the life of his Son.

Friend, regardless of the strength of your faith, the burdens you carry, the pain you endure, the temptations you battle, the doubts you're trying to push aside, or the grief that's left a gaping hole in your heart, you aren't alone. There's a place for you here. So don't leave your humanity at the door, but in the pages ahead let our Lord Jesus infuse comfort and strength into every ounce of your being.

Wherever you find yourself right now, rest assured, he will meet you there.

With love,
Kristen and Sarah

PART 1

WEAKNESS

1

When You Despise Your Weakness

Hebrews 4:15

I'm going to take a long shot here and assume that you, the one holding this book in your hands, are a living, breathing *human*. I may not know much else about you, but I do know this: You are not a random blob of atoms thrown together by chance. You have a heart that pumps with precision, lungs that rise and fall with each breath, emotions that ebb and flow, a mind that thinks, and a face that resembles some others but is entirely unique.

You and I are profoundly complex—body, mind, and soul—intricate beyond what the brightest minds can comprehend. And yet, whether or not we like to admit it, we're also painfully limited and dependent beings. Without air, we cease breathing. Without precise electrical pulses, our hearts stop beating. Without proper immune systems, microscopic germs wreak havoc. We're vulnerable to the world around us and at war with the passions within us. Our earthly frames are carefully and intentionally designed yet fragile to the core—exposed and battered by the elements of a sin-ravaged world and fractured by weakness, sin, and suffering.

The irony is, we invest endless resources trying to convince ourselves we're something we're not. We strive to delay aging and the dreaded reality that death will one day knock on our door. We equate self-sufficiency with a life well lived. And we spend our whole lives searching for meaning and striving for what's lasting, while running from the very One who holds both in his hands.

It's exhausting, isn't it?

Like a hamster on a wheel, we run ourselves ragged, avoiding anything that reminds us of how temporal and not in control we really are.

WEAKNESS ISN'T OUR ENEMY

I imagine you've arrived at this section on weakness with one of two perspectives. Maybe you feel your limitations acutely because of physical challenges or other heavy circumstances that have sucked your capacity dry. You're reminded of your weaknesses around every corner.

Or maybe you feel pretty good about life right now, confident in who you are and what you've accomplished. You may not *feel* particularly weak, but you have a chronic, low-grade fear that you're one mistake or calamity away from losing everything you've worked so hard to achieve.

Whether you're plagued with weakness or running from it, eventually you'll have to face your humanity head-on.

Eventually, we all wonder, *Where did I go wrong? Why can't I get it together?* If you're a Christian, you're faced with even deeper questions: *If God truly loves me, why does he allow me to struggle in the first place? Is he patient toward my limitations, or is he annoyed by my weaknesses and failings?*

Thankfully, we don't have to wonder.

FORCED TO DIG DEEPER

Several years ago, trials came like unrelenting waves. Chronic illness knocked me down every day, and on top of that, disappointment and struggle kept crashing on my family. First, my husband lost his job, draining our finances as the needs multiplied. To make matters worse, our young son's neurodiverse challenges worsened by the day, and in my weariness, I pleaded with God to show me his favor and compassion. I was desperate for reassurance that he truly cared about me and what our family was walking through. But what followed was *not* the answer I was hoping for.

Not long after we'd taken our son to a long-awaited specialist whom we'd been referred to, we learned this medical practice was impersonating the *actual* specialist we thought we were seeing. They had duped dozens of desperate families like ours in the process. By the time the truth came to light, we were out thousands of dollars and could no longer afford to see the real specialist. It hit like a gut punch, and in all honesty, God didn't just feel absent—he felt cruel.

As I scoured the Scriptures, desperate for a lifeline to keep my head above the waves, simplistic Christian slogans that once made sense now seemed to taunt me: *Just have faith and trust that it will all work out. God won't give you more than you can handle. There's a good purpose to all this.*

Even true statements like "God is good" are easy to believe when circumstances match our idea of goodness. But what do we do when life falls apart and disrupts what once made sense?

We're forced to dig deeper.

The moment we're tempted to pull back from Jesus is the very moment we must lean in. Because if we look closely at the life of Christ, we'll encounter the very nature and character of God. Not only are we sinners who need a Savior; we're also sufferers who need a Comforter and Redeemer.

There are times, however, we may know this in our heads, but for some reason, it hits a brick wall at the heart level. Usually, it's when we find ourselves at a crossroads between *knowing* the truth about God and *staking* our entire life on it. This point often comes when life unravels and our perception of God is shaken to the core.

For example, until our faith is tested, we're more likely to rest our confidence on simplistic interpretations of God's promises in passages like Matthew 7:9–11: "Which of you, if your son asks for bread, will give him a stone? Or if he asks for a fish, will give him a snake? If you, then, though you are evil, know how to give good gifts to your children, how much more will your Father in heaven give good gifts to those who ask him!" (NIV).

I don't know about you, but my interpretation of "bread and fish" usually corresponds to what seems good to me at the moment. Therefore, when God acts outside the bounds of those perceptions, it feels like he's giving me a stone or a snake.

If you find yourself at that crossroads right now, you're in good company. The pages of this book stem from a deeply rooted desire to grasp how God is both powerful *and* personal—how he's *really* for us. And there's no greater way to see the heart of God than to see it lived out through the life of Jesus.

WHY JESUS'S HUMANITY AND DEITY BOTH MATTER

Think about a past or present difficulty in your life. When it comes to suffering or disappointment, how do you and I tend to respond? Naturally, we want out. We avoid it at all costs or push it to our mental back burner—believing the path *around* pain and weakness is what's best for us.

Now consider Jesus. Unlike us, he *willingly* left the comforts and glories of heaven and became human. He did this fully aware of the suffering he would endure on our behalf. It defies logic: Why would a loving Father send his Son into a harsh world to save those who hate him? It sounds a lot like a father giving his son a stone or a snake.

Yes, God could have left us to ourselves—to the consequences of our own rebellious hearts and the pain that comes from living in a fallen world. But he didn't. He is Immanuel, God with us. His love took on human form in Jesus.

Here's what's striking to me: Jesus could have descended to earth as a thirty-year-old man, begun his three years of ministry, and died on the cross as the sacrifice for our sins. But he didn't. Instead, he came into the world as we all do, dependent on earthly parents, enduring the full limitations and pain of humanity. He willingly chose this path. Why?

Because Jesus needed to experience the full extent of our humanity in order to redeem it.

Therefore, we must hold Jesus's humanity and deity carefully together. If we lose sight of his deity, we reduce him to a sympathetic man who is powerless to save. If we lose sight of his humanity, we have a God who can save but who lacks firsthand experience of the realities of this fallen world.

So it's the profound truth of both Jesus's humanity and his deity that gives us both eternal and present hope. He isn't distant, uncaring, or out of touch. He feels what we feel. He knows the full extent of the human experience—even to the point of death. He knows the full scale of suffering this world brings.

And yet Jesus doesn't stop at forgiving our sins and comforting our sorrows. He draws near. He gives us his Holy Spirit, not only to strengthen and comfort us in our humanity . . . but also to redeem it.

WHAT MAKES YOU HUMAN

Weakness is a constant reminder of our finiteness. We aren't unbreakable. We aren't infallible. And we certainly have to depend on people besides ourselves.

In other words, we aren't God.

But consider this: Maybe God isn't as disappointed and frustrated by our weaknesses as we are. In fact, maybe God knows that our determination to avoid weakness is actually a greater threat to us than weakness itself. He knows that we only hurt ourselves by trying to live as if we were made to be independent, when he designed us to be creatures dependent on him for all things.

As humans, we rely on sleep. Without it, we grow tired. We rely on nourishment for our bodies to function effectively. In sickness and injury, we're often dependent on medicine, treatment, and the wisdom of others. As Christians, we rely on knowing the truth of the Bible in order to recognize deception in a world full of lies. And above all, we're dependent on God not only for eternal salvation but also for the very breath that sustains our life one moment at a time.

You and I aren't disappointments or failures because we're inherently limited by our humanity. We're simply human, designed to be dependent on the One who created us.

Therefore, because Jesus walked this earth as a limited being, he has compassion toward us, knowing what it's like to give up his unlimited deity and take on the limitations and weaknesses of a human frame.

> We do not have a high priest who is unable to empathize with our weaknesses, but we have one who has been tempted in every way, just as we are—yet he did not sin. (Hebrews 4:15, NIV)

Not only does Jesus know your weakness, he also empathizes with it. Not only does he have compassion toward your weakness, he is also able and willing to draw near to you with his strength.

WEAKNESS IS THE BEGINNING OF STRENGTH

Friend, we won't always understand the "why" behind God's ways or be able to make sense of the limitations that hinder us from the life we long for, but we can be confident in this: Jesus loved us enough to become human and endure the pain of this world. He knew he'd be forsaken by his Father, while suffering the most horrendous death we could imagine, to call us his own. For "greater love has no one than this: to lay down one's life for one's friends" (John 15:13, NIV).

Your limitations don't push God away. They are exactly what lead you to the One who has everything you need. As we'll see in the chapters ahead, Jesus is drawn to needy people. Until you see your weakness, you can't receive the strength of Jesus.

Do you feel weak today? I know I do.

Jesus invites us, "Come to me, all you who are weary and burdened, and I will give you rest. Take my yoke upon you and learn from me, for I am gentle and humble in heart, and you will find rest for your souls" (Matthew 11:28–29, NIV).

Though we may not always understand his ways, because of Jesus, we can know without a doubt that the heart of God is for us—breathing hope and redemption into every facet of our humanity, including the weaknesses we so often despise.

Meeting with Jesus

1. How have you responded to your weaknesses and limitations lately? Have they led you toward shame, embarrassment, self-accusation, or anger, or have they led you to lean on Jesus as your strength?
2. Why does our world despise weakness? How does acknowledging your weakness lead to freedom?
3. How would your relationship with Jesus change if you fully believed he empathizes with you? Read 2 Corinthians 12:9. Write or pray your thoughts, questions, or concerns to the Lord and ask for his grace in each one.

2

When It's Hard to Be Human

John 1:14

Why is it so hard to be human?

Have you ever thought about this? We rarely consider an answer because our humanity is innate, inbuilt, assumed. Day in and day out, you live with yourself, in your own skin. You wake up in the morning, eat, drink, talk, reason, make decisions, feel emotions, work, play, go to sleep, and then do it all over again. The habit of humanity feels normal, even mundane at times—so mundane that we hardly think about it. We just *are*.

But in the next breath, we hesitate. We realize we are complex creatures. Humans are a complicated and beautiful melting pot of confusion, hope, realism, burden, trauma, and happiness—all at once.

To be sure, our humanity is a bittersweet affair.

When my immune system turned on me fifteen years ago, I woke up to my need. Health, which once seemed like a given, suddenly became uncertain. What about you? Where does life weigh on you? Perhaps it's that pain you can't shake. The relationship that went bad. The past that still haunts you. The once-sharp mind that now can't remember names. The searing grief of loss. The toils of work, the scarcity of time, or the demands of loved ones.

In a book about Jesus drawing near to us, we have to start here, with what it actually means to be human. *Who are we? And why does this matter?* We need to better understand what we're made of to catch a glimpse of what God might be up to. And in the beginning, Scripture tells us this: God made us in his image (Genesis 1:26–27), and he made us *very* good (verse 31). No matter what you're going through right now, whether you're in a place of pain or abundance, life-altering disruptions or small ones, every reader of this book has one thing in common.

You are a living, breathing picture of God.

Like a mirror, you reflect the divine image. This is what makes you different from your dog or cat, the birds outside your window, the fish in the sea, and the cattle on a thousand hills. It's what sets you apart from the sunsets you wonder at, the natural disasters you balk at, the skies and waters you explore. Only humans reflect God, the Creator of all things, the Maker of heaven and earth. When you stop to think about this, it's an astounding reality—and a confusing one.

Being made in God's image means we look a lot like him.

And it means we are *not* him.

LIKE GOD—AND UNLIKE HIM

According to my mom, when I was about three years old, I looked at her, eyes wide, and said, "I get it! I'm not you—I'm *me*!"

Something similar is true about us and our Creator.

First, we look a lot like God. We are relational and rational beings with the ability to reason, emote, and communicate with other humans. We have souls, meaning we have eternity planted within our hearts (Ecclesiastes 3:11), the capacity to live forever and long for it, and this is what sets us apart from the rest of God's creation.[1]

We are also like God in our capabilities (though different from him). We create, rule over creation, make plans, pronounce judgments, and organize as God has brought order—all because God said, "Let us make man in our image, after our likeness" (Genesis 1:26). And so it was. We look a lot like him.

But we are also *not* like him.

Only God is . . . God. He alone is divine, the great I AM (Exodus 3:14; Isaiah 44:6–7; 46:9). Unlike some religions that believe we can become gods, the Bible says that God exists within his own category: "Know therefore today, and lay it to your heart, that the LORD is God in heaven above and on the earth beneath; there is no other" (Deuteronomy 4:39). We're going to see throughout this book how God delights to make us more like him, how he restores the mirror image that has been marred and broken by sin. But even then, we are still mirrors. And a mirror can never actually become what it reflects. God is entirely other than us.

Only God exists for himself. Only God defies logic and limits. Only God has no needs because he is uncreated, unparalleled, and perfectly, wholly content in himself. Only God deserves all devotion from all creatures in heaven and on earth. "From him and through him and to him are all things. To him be glory forever. Amen" (Romans 11:36). This is simply who he is, and in these ways, he is not like us.

And yet this same God chose to become like us in every way.[2]

He chose to become a weak human being.

THE CREATOR BECAME LIKE THE CREATURE

You may read that and think, *Why? Why would such a holy and powerful and* other *God—so limitless, so awesome, so perfect in every way—become like me? Why lay it all aside for a situation that seems far less than God's ideal?*

John's gospel gives us insight: "He came to his own, and his own people did not receive him. But to all who did receive him, who believed in his name, he gave the right to become children of God, who were born, not of blood nor of the will of the flesh nor of the will of man, but of God" (1:11–13).

Your Creator became like you so you will become like him.*

But we need to back up a bit. Before we can grasp the implications of God "[coming] to his own," let's put ourselves in the shoes of John's original hearers. The opening line of his gospel reads, "In the beginning was the Word" (verse 1). His readers would have immediately thought of the creation story, where Moses writes, "In the beginning . . ." (Genesis 1:1). In other words, a new beginning is dawning. God is doing something entirely fresh that builds on something as ancient as Adam.

When Adam and Eve sinned in the garden—when beauty and delight turned sour because of their disobedience—God's image in humanity was fouled up, marred, spoiled. Not just for them, but for us too. If we're honest, we know this is true. We can't go one day without making a mess of things, even if that mess is neatly concealed in our minds and hearts. God made Adam from the dust; this was very good (Genesis 1:31; 2:7). But because of Adam's sin, he would someday return to dust and every person after him would too (Genesis 3:19; Romans 5:12–14). The dust that once meant life for us now means death.

This is why Jesus became like us.

"The Word became flesh and dwelt among us" (John 1:14).

For John's original audience, the idea of the Creator of all things, the Word of life, becoming flesh would have seemed preposterous, even blasphemous. God is entirely *other* than us, as we've seen. How could he possibly become *like* us? But he did. So that we could be-

---

* Only God is fully divine, of course, and in that way we will never become like him. Keep reading to the end of this chapter to see what John, the gospel writer, means by this astonishing truth.

come like him—sinless, faultless, and restored to the mirror image of God.

Adam's sin devastated our humanity, but the sinlessness of Jesus would heal us.

TWO KINDS OF WEAKNESS

This means a few things for us.

In a world full of humans who desperately want to be "like God" (Genesis 3:5), a world that demands a "you got this" mentality and superhuman capacity, the incarnation of Jesus shouts a different message: God doesn't expect you to be more than he created you to be. Your *created weakness* is very good.

God purposefully made Adam and Eve with limitations so they would find joy in depending on him. Yes, *joy*. The fact that you are not God is *good* for you because trying to be God will only crush you. Jesus lived out his created weakness perfectly, and what did this look like? Dependence on his Father: "Truly, truly, I say to you, the Son can do nothing of his own accord, but only what he sees the Father doing" (John 5:19). Don't apologize for your created weakness; embrace it. God isn't embarrassed by who you are. He loves the way he made you—so much that Jesus took on the very same frame.

This also means that God deeply cares about *consequential weakness:* what sin has corrupted. Why do bees sting? Why do viruses invade? Why do earthquakes destroy? Why do our bodies age, break down, and eventually return to dust? Remember, Adam's sin devastated our humanity. Because of this, we often confuse sin's consequences with our created weakness, apologizing for what God created as good and excusing what God would never call good. But God doesn't excuse sin or its effects. Instead, he deals with it in the person of Jesus.

"To all who did receive [Jesus], who believed in his name, he gave the right to become children of God, who were born, not of blood nor of the will of the flesh nor of the will of man, but of God" (John 1:12–13).

Jesus was born as a human so we could be born again into God's family.

Jesus, the perfect mirror image of God, took on flesh to redeem our flesh.

Jesus became like us so we will become like him.

FROM HEAVEN HE CAME AND SOUGHT US

In our fallen world, it's easy to think God doesn't care. He feels so removed, so far from our frailty. But the coming of his Son into this fallen world, wrapped in our flesh, tells a different story. It's as if God has been seeking us just like he sought Adam and Eve after they sinned: "Where are you?" (Genesis 3:9). He has sought us even when we have rejected him. We're the ones who haven't cared, who have strong-armed God in an attempt to prove ourselves capable apart from him. But God came for us anyway, laying aside his rights as God (Philippians 2:6–7), to draw near to us—to validate his good creation and restore what's been lost.

We need a Savior who knows our weakness.

Jesus, the Second Adam, does.

From heaven he came and sought us. Through dust he came to redeem us.

Meeting with Jesus

1. Read all of Genesis 3. In what ways has our world been ravaged by sin? In what ways do you feel its effect on you—both struggles within and circumstances around you?
2. Do you struggle more with the belief that Jesus was fully divine or that he was fully human? How has that affected how you view him?
3. Journal all the ways you feel your status as dust and thank God that he became like you so that he could make a way to redeem those very things.

3

When Nothing Seems to Calm Your Anxious Thoughts

Matthew 6:25–34

I flipped back and forth on the creaky hotel bed, trying to tune out the obnoxious hum of the air conditioner as it sputtered and clanked like the engine of an old pickup truck. It was working just as hard to pump out air as I was to drown it out, but my attempts were futile. The more I tried to distract myself, the more it was all I could hear. For brief moments, the noise faded into the background of my mind, but eventually, I had to surrender to the fact that all I could do was anxiously wait for relief to arrive with the dawn.

For many of us, anxiety functions a lot like that annoying motor, keeping us tossing and turning at night with a clenched jaw and inner angst. Over time, we may become so used to living with a chronic low-grade level of anxiety that it becomes second nature.

For others, anxiety becomes an all-consuming presence that affects every sphere of life. Sometimes consciously, oftentimes subconsciously. Whatever camp you may find yourself in (or if, like me, you fluctuate between both), you've likely heard one or more of these phrases:

> "Stop worrying about what you can't control."
> "Have you prayed about it?"
> "Quit dwelling on it and try to change your mindset."

While there is a nugget of truth in each, they're too simplistic.

Thankfully, Jesus wasn't silent on the issue of anxiety. He knew it would be part of living in a world of uncertainty and struggle. The fact that he addressed the anxious hearts of his listeners two thousand years ago should comfort us: We aren't the first and we won't be the last. Listen to Jesus's words to us in Matthew 6:

> Therefore I tell you, do not be anxious about your life, what you will eat or what you will drink, nor about your body, what you will put on. . . . Look at the birds of the air: they neither sow nor reap nor gather into barns, and yet your heavenly Father feeds them. Are you not of more value than they? . . . Therefore do not be anxious. . . . For the Gentiles seek after all these things, and your heavenly Father knows that you need them all. But seek first the kingdom of God and his righteousness, and all these things will be added to you.
>
> Therefore do not be anxious about tomorrow, for tomorrow will be anxious for itself. Sufficient for the day is its own trouble. (verses 25–26, 31–34)

Jesus doesn't curtly tell us, "Suck it up, buttercup," as if he's impatiently tapping his foot, waiting for us to get it together. No, as one who walked this earth, he knows we have plenty of reasons to be anxious when looking at the world around us.

Instead, he tells us *why* we don't need to be consumed by countless anxiety-inducing realities: We aren't left to our own resources. He loves us, knows exactly what we need, and is faithful to provide it.

It sounds simple, doesn't it? But we all know it's far easier to believe these truths in our heads than it is to practically apply them. To receive the comfort of Jesus's words, we need to accurately hear his heart for us.

Is Jesus speaking to every anxious feeling we might experience in our physical beings, or is he referring to the worries of life that rob us of the peace he offers? Let's begin by distinguishing the two forms of anxiety we can experience.

ANXIETY FROM WEAKNESS

According to the *Oxford English Dictionary,* anxiety is "a feeling of worry, nervousness, or unease, typically about an imminent event or something with an uncertain outcome."[1]

We all know the feeling.

But before we delve into the common struggle of anxiety, we need to make an important distinction: Anxiety that stems from human unbelief is *not* always the same as anxiety that stems from human weakness.

We live in a world broken by sin, with bodies and minds affected by that reality. I've seen firsthand how trauma, illnesses, and physical deficiencies can cause our bodies to respond to stimuli even when our souls know better. We may rack our brains and plead for God to reveal some hidden sin of unbelief, but sometimes, despite prayer and wise counsel, anxiety isn't solely a spiritual issue (even though there are always spiritual dynamics at work).

The fact is, we really aren't in control of much at all, including how our hormones fluctuate, our nerves fire, our neurotransmitters react to microscopic invaders, or our reflexes operate. And yet we live most days under the delusion of control.

Anxiety actually brings us closer to the reality that we have no control—a truth that's unbearable without the knowledge that God is with us and over all things. I've come to believe some weaknesses are really mercies that draw us toward active faith—an in-the-moment reliance on the God who *is* in control.

But we cannot dismiss the fact that, at times, overwhelming anxiety can stem from physiological causes. It's a genuine form of suffering. And I believe the Lord shows compassion and mercy toward those who are plagued by it.

However, weakness in our humanity does *not* give us an excuse to live as victims with no personal responsibility or hope of change. Although we aren't promised healing on this side of heaven, God is always able. It's wise to still take steps to best care for our bodies and improve our situations, even if by degrees. However, I can testify that even if he doesn't fully free us from our inner turmoil, Jesus is still at work within it as we lean on him. Only with the Spirit's help is it possible to experience a level of spiritual peace and rest amid feelings of physical and mental unrest.

If this *isn't* a struggle you've experienced, thank God for that. But remember to be patient with those who may experience burdens you haven't been called to bear. Just because we don't understand something doesn't mean it doesn't exist. Personally, in my battle against Lyme disease and my child's lifelong battle with neurological challenges, I've seen the difference between anxiety rooted in unbelief and anxiety rooted in a dysregulated body that's been affected by the Fall.

Both stem from weakness—but one is from the heart; the other is from living in a frame riddled with cracks.

ANXIETY FROM UNBELIEF

How, then, do we make sense of the common form of anxiety that Jesus was speaking of? Kelly Kapic, in his book *You're Only Human*, gives some helpful insights:

> Anxiety is the emotional response that tells us that *we are not enough.* If God comes to mind, anxiety tells us either that God is not enough or that he doesn't care.
>
> Rather than allowing you to be honest about your finitude, your anxiety tells you that not only should you be able to do everything you imagine needs to be done, but you should do it perfectly. Anxiety whispers in your ear not that you are a good creature made by God but that you are insignificant, a disappointment, even a failure. Anxiety confuses limitation with sin, thus convincing us that we are letting God down.[2]

He's right. Some of our anxieties stem from trying to live beyond the natural limitations God's given us. We tend to see limitations as challenges to be conquered rather than gifts given by God for our good. When we hit limits that frustrate us—fatigue, hunger, sickness, forgetfulness, time—we want God to remove them rather than help us live within the healthy boundaries he's created.

Another common cause of anxiety, however, isn't as much resistance to our limitations as it is fear of what we can't control.

> We worry this month's paycheck won't cover the unexpected medical bills.
> Our stomach ties in knots as we await test results.
> We obsessively ruminate over how others perceive us.

We're gripped by fear over tragedies we can't foresee, children we can't fully protect, and threats to livelihood, safety, and freedom.

The list is endless. But so are the promises we have through Jesus.

ANXIOUS . . . FOR WHAT?

Stop for a moment and take a personal inventory of what causes you anxiety. Can you pinpoint anything specific?

The Lord knows what you and I need, and he promises to provide it—even if not in our timing or way. However, what if much of our anxiety comes from what we *want*, not what we need?

It's not a coincidence that the Matthew 6 passage we read opens with the word *therefore*. Jesus intended those verses to be understood in light of what he had just spoken to his listeners: "Don't store up for yourselves treasures on earth, where moth and rust destroy and where thieves break in and steal. But store up for yourselves treasures in heaven . . . for where your treasure is, there your heart will be also" (Matthew 6:19–21, CSB).

Are we anxious because we don't have what we need? Or are we anxious because we don't have what we want—what our hearts are set on having in this world, even if Jesus knows it's not what's best for us?

He may not give us the object of our desire, but he promises to give us what we most need when we surrender to his plan: peace, joy, and contentment—even if by degrees. "Seek first the kingdom of God and his righteousness, and all these things will be added to you" (verse 33). When Jesus is our greatest joy, every undeserved blessing he gives becomes something we can enjoy without fear of losing it. And everything he withholds will no longer keep us in the grip of anxiety, because our joy is no longer dependent on it.

RECOGNIZE AND REPLACE

We can't always control what comes into our minds, but we *can* control how we respond to it (2 Corinthians 10:5). How, then, do we take our anxious thoughts captive and reorient them with the promises of Jesus in these scriptures? We recognize unbelief and replace it with truth.

Here are a few practical examples:

Anxious thought: I fear what others think of me.

Unbelief: God's opinion of me doesn't matter as much as the opinion of others. Therefore, I am the sum of my choices, successes, failures, and reputation.

Truth: My joy, identity, and value are not determined by the opinion of others or my successes and failures. Jesus loves me enough to die for me and provide for me.

Jesus says to you: "Therefore I tell you, do not be anxious about your life, what you will eat or what you will drink, nor about your body, what you will put on. Is not life more than food, and the body more than clothing? . . . Seek first the kingdom of God and his righteousness, and all these things will be added to you" (Matthew 6:25, 33).

Anxious thought: I worry about my financial future. How in the world will my needs be met?

Unbelief: God can't or won't provide for my needs (or what I think I need), because I see no earthly way out of this situation.

Truth: God knows what I need and has promised to provide. He may not provide in the timing or way I expect, but he can't break his promises.

Jesus encourages you: "Look at the birds of the air: they neither sow nor reap nor gather into barns, and yet your heavenly Father feeds them. Are you not of more value than they?" (Matthew 6:26).

Anxious thought: I'm gripped by fear over all the bad things that might happen to me and those I love.

Unbelief: God isn't in control of every detail, so I can't trust that he'll keep me or those I love from harm. I'm at the mercy of chance, and it's up to me to guard our lives.

Truth: God holds our days in his hands. Nothing can harm me or those I love apart from his good purposes for our lives.

Jesus asks you: "Which of you by being anxious can add a single hour to his span of life?" (Matthew 6:27).

Anxious thought: I'm worried about how I'm going to get everything done tomorrow.

Unbelief: Peace is found only in knowing what the future holds.

Truth: Peace is found in trusting the One who holds tomorrow in his hands and who promises to equip me for everything that lies ahead if I depend on him one step at a time.

Jesus reminds you: "Therefore do not be anxious about tomorrow, for tomorrow will be anxious for itself. Sufficient for the day is its own trouble" (Matthew 6:34).

Friend, you and I are vulnerable to anxiety because we're limited beings with little control over what happens in our lives. We may not be able to control everything that comes into our minds, and we may not always recognize the source of our anxious feelings. But we have a Savior who intricately knows us and wants to set us free from anxiety—even if incrementally. We cast our worries on him not only because he can do something about them but also because he wholeheartedly, unequivocally cares for us (1 Peter 5:6–7).

Today come to Jesus honestly and ask him to give you insight into the anxiety that's robbing you of peace. We may not know the needed tools to tune our anxious hearts, but Jesus does. He is ready and able to offer you the rest that can be found only in him.

Meeting with Jesus

1. What causes your anxiety to rise the most? Pinpoint a few areas and write them down in a journal.
2. What is the typical by-product of anxiety for you? Control, anger, tears, or avoidance? Why do you think this is the case?
3. Do any of these by-products stem from the wrong belief that God won't protect or provide for you? Write promises from Matthew 6:25–34 in response to your unbelief and pray for God's help to fight it with truth.

4

When You Have Nothing Left to Give

Mark 12:41–44

"Why do you hurt all the time, Mom?"

My kids ask why I can't do the things other people can do—and honestly, I find myself asking the Lord the same question. It can feel confusing, even unsettling, that he has called me into realms of service that highlight the weakest parts of me.

Do you know what it's like to give from a place of emptiness? To take one more step, wondering if what you have is enough for others and even for God?

For years, I have struggled with neuropathy from a chronic autoimmune condition. I write this using my non-dominant hand, while my bad arm sits limp, pulsing with pain. I turn my head to glance across the room, and the tenderness in my jaw and neck reminds me how a simple gesture for one person can be a laborious feat for another. Every day, I am painfully aware of my fallen frame.

So is Jesus. He sees—and he knows.

THE ONE WHO KNOWS YOUR HEART

One day, Mark tells us, after teaching in the temple, "[Jesus] sat down opposite the treasury and watched the people putting money into the offering box. Many rich people put in large sums. And a poor widow came and put in two small copper coins, which make a penny" (Mark 12:41–42).

Striking, isn't it? Jesus wasn't casually strolling by the offering on his way somewhere else. No—he planted himself across from it and *watched.* Think of a parent who takes a moment to watch their kids play, or a police officer who idles in a parking lot, eyeing the road. Both observe for a purpose: to respond to a need with instruction, correction, or encouragement. Jesus observed for a purpose too.

Not only does he see our movements, he also knows our deepest motivations.

He notices *you,* friend. Our near and always-present God cares about you, your circumstances, and the condition of your heart before him. And God's knowledge of you isn't generalized and detached information, the way we say we know our president or prime minister. His knowledge is total, detailed, *personal.* He knows us because he sees everything about us.

Including what's in our hearts.

He knows the grieving parents who keep serving at church even though their hearts are broken.

He knows the full-time employee who feels buried and overwhelmed by responsibilities.

He knows the suffering mind, oppressed by dark and shaming thoughts, who wakes up to another day and still chooses to do the next thing.

Just as Jesus knew the poor widow, who gave two copper coins—a pittance to some but an outpouring to him.

The story of the widow's offering comforts me, not only because we share a common, limited humanity, but also because of God's nearness to us in *his* humanity. He sees, he knows—and he is near.

Yet Jesus's closeness can be a terrifying thing. He is God, after all.

OFFERING OURSELVES TO GOD

The world may tell us, "You're enough," but somewhere deep inside us we know we aren't—especially before the watchful eyes of our holy and perfect God. Think about it: Can any one of us say that we have done everything God commands? We're challenged by this question in Mark 12, right before Jesus sat down in the temple. He had been talking with a scribe who asked him, "Which commandment is the most important of all?" (verse 28). Jesus answered him,

> The most important is, "Hear, O Israel: The Lord our God, the Lord is one. And you shall love the Lord your God with all your heart and with all your soul and with all your mind and with all your strength." The second is this: "You shall love your neighbor as yourself." There is no other commandment greater than these. (verses 29–31)

Jesus was talking about a perfect love for God and others. *Gulp.* Guilty. If we say we've fulfilled God's law of love, we're lying. On our best days, we know our sincere efforts are laced with self-preoccupation and vainglory. And on our worst ones, we know we're just getting by with lip service and spiritual masquerades. The Lord is well aware of our instinctual ploys to procure his favor—all the self-centered antics we pull to be enough in his sight.

How many of us resist our weaknesses because they expose our humanity? How many of us expect to gain God's favor through what we do and what we're able to give—but then are shocked to discover his favor comes only to the needy?

Friend, we are not enough before God. Not on our own, at least. We are exposed as spiritually impoverished before his eyes—our sin having robbed us (Genesis 3:7; Hebrews 4:13). Yet the One who watches us, observing our affections and innermost motives, is the One who also fulfilled God's law of love—perfectly and without limitations. *Why would he do this?* So that all our messed-up, sin-laced motives—our entire account of wrong before God—would be cleared. So that *we* would be covered.

What a relief that the watchful Judge of every person is also our near Savior. The One who meets us right where we are is the One who emptied himself of limitless heavenly glory to be hemmed into human skin. *He* is the One who observes us, who knows our every desire, motive, thought, and deed—not to condemn us, but to cover us. "You know the grace of our Lord Jesus Christ, that though he was rich, yet for your sake he became poor, so that you by his poverty might become rich" (2 Corinthians 8:9).

Just when we realize we can't possibly offer anything to God, there he is, offering himself to us. And it's from this place of security in Christ that we're able to freely offer ourselves to others, no matter how they respond.

WHAT YOU HAVE ISN'T ENOUGH

Here's one truth that comforts me when I feel my lack: Jesus gave everything from his fullness (John 1:16; Colossians 1:19)—and it still wasn't enough to meet the demands of those around him.

Now, don't get me wrong: Jesus was, and is, enough. What I mean is that people didn't see this. They were blind to his glory, deaf to his word, and hardened to his mission.

He performed miracles, but some witnesses "begged him to leave their region" (Matthew 8:34) while power-hungry religious leaders rejected him: "If we let him go on like this, everyone will believe in him" (John 11:48). He rebuked his own disciple who couldn't understand his purpose: "Get behind me, Satan!" (Mark 8:33). He disappointed his family: "Not even his brothers believed in him" (John 7:5).

Even at the moment of his greatest offering, he couldn't satisfy onlookers who mocked, "He saved others; let him save himself" (Luke 23:35).

Jesus gave everything—and *is* everything—but it still wasn't enough for people.

So, when my kids ask about why my body hurts, when my limits disappoint them, I remember that Jesus understands me. He knows what it's like to sincerely serve others—and still come up short in their eyes.

What can we do when people criticize us, opportunity passes us by, or health fails us? Can we trust God even with our weakness, believing that our meager offerings are treasured by him, even if they're misunderstood or dismissed by the world?

What a comfort for us when our offerings aren't enough in the world's sight. When we wonder if anyone cares about all we're giving, *Jesus does.* He can see what people can't—the motives of our hearts. He can see how we truly want to honor and please him with what little we have. He sees our little offering, given in faithfulness.

What about you? Like the widow in the story, perhaps you have known extreme circumstances and stretching limitations. Widows in Jesus's day and culture were defined by grief, vulnerability, and loneliness. You may not be a widow, but you know vulnerability and the deep trust in God it requires. You know what it means to walk by faith that God will see your needs and provide for you—not necessarily as you *want* him to, but as he knows is best.

The little you offer to the Lord in faithfulness, friend, is an abundance in his sight. God's desire for the weak and weary is that our hearts are turned toward him in all we do, no matter how small our offerings may appear. *Do we love him? And is love for him and our neighbor the motivation for everything we offer?*

Looking to Jesus, we behold one who *is* God yet who gave everything he had—all he had to live on. Why? To fill up our emptiness with the promise of his very life, his fullness.

THE BEAUTY OF EMPTY

If your weakness feels defeating, it might sound idealistic to talk about Jesus making much out of your little. All you see is the meagerness of the moment. So how does Jesus's fullness provide for our emptiness? And how does this good news help us trust him with the sacrifices we make?

God will redirect your motives. "Whatever you do, work heartily, as for the Lord and not for men" (Colossians 3:23). When Jesus turns our hearts to himself in faith, he frees us from selfish motivations—even little by little. Whether I'm parenting my kids in private or sharing my words in public, I often struggle with wrong motives. But Jesus is increasingly teaching me how to serve him, not my own name. Ask yourself, *Why am I doing what I'm doing? If no one but Jesus were watching, would I still be motivated to serve him?* Believing that his value system is different from the world's, you can give joyfully from your lack and trust him with the outcome.

God will use your sacrifices. "With a freewill offering I will sacrifice to you" (Psalm 54:6). Jesus measures what we offer him not by quantity but by cost. Even when we can't see how, nothing is wasted when it's given to God. Not only does God transform our hearts as he draws us nearer to his fullness; he also works in the hearts of those around us. A friend recently shared about her dying sister in Christ whose sacrifice of joy spoke so loudly to the hospital staff, they commented on how different her room felt. The world may take notice of *us* in earthly success and self-sufficiency, but the world will take notice of *Christ* when they see otherworldly strength and joy flowing from our emptiness.

God will teach you to rest. "Come to me, all who labor and are heavy laden, and I will give you rest" (Matthew 11:28). When our confidence is in what we have to offer, we frantically strive to maintain the fragile facade of our self-worth, leading to a pendulum swing between insecurity and pride. But when our security is in Christ, we are freed from the tyranny of striving and find rest in his acceptance. Why? Because he has *declared* us enough, not because of our efforts to *prove* we're enough. We find our rest in his perfection rather than in our performance.

God will reward your faithfulness. "Well done, good and faithful servant" (Matthew 25:21). At the end of our days, Jesus, our judge, will pronounce a verdict on how we spent our lives. Like the widow, when we "put in everything [we have], all [we have] to live on" (Mark 12:44) and trust our souls into Jesus's capable grip, we won't come up empty. We will fully and finally have everything we need to live on, now and into eternity (Matthew 19:29). So don't hold anything back from the Lord, friend. Give yourself to him, no matter how empty you feel, and let his secure commendation and his perfect provision put your weary heart at ease: "Well done, well done."

Meeting with Jesus

1. How do you respond when you come up against your limitations? What does this reveal about the motivations of your heart?
2. If you truly believed Jesus is pleased with your meager offerings, how would this change your day-to-day life? How would it change your view of God? Your view of yourself? Write out and try to memorize Isaiah 40:29 this week.
3. How can you encourage someone struggling with weakness and disappointment and point them to Jesus?

5

When You Feel Like You Don't Measure Up

Luke 9:46–48

I recently learned about bummer lambs. At first glance, the explanation is just as depressing as you'd expect. But in God's created world, there's always more than what meets the eye.

Occasionally, a ewe will give birth to a lamb and reject it, sometimes due to a defect or weakness in the lamb, other times for no clear reason. It's been said, "These little lambs will hang their heads so low that it looks like something is wrong with its neck. Their spirit is broken."[1]

If the shepherd doesn't step in, the poor "bummer lamb" will slowly die. Therefore, the shepherd will take the helpless little bummer into his home and tenderly care for it until it's strong enough to live with the flock.

But even once it's grown, the lamb will never forget the sound of its shepherd's voice. It will be the first to draw near when he calls. "It is not that the bummer lamb is loved more, it just knows intimately the one who loves it."[2]

I'm struck by the poetic picture this real-life scenario paints for us. Much like in the world's value system, the flock (and even the lamb's own mother) looks down on this little lamb. He's the weak link among the strong.

The irony is, this poor bummer was pushed away by those who were, in fact, of no greater value than him. And yet, as he stands dejected and alone, the neediness that pushed others away is the very thing that draws the shepherd close. Is the rejection of the others a reflection of his worth? No, the shepherd's personal and tender care for the bummer lamb is the true reflection of his value.

The once-dejected lamb now stands with confidence among the others—not because he's the greatest or most deserving, but because he knows he's intimately loved and protected by his shepherd. His value is determined not by his own greatness but by the greatness of his shepherd's love.

THE WORLD'S VALUE SYSTEM

Most of us have felt like the bummer lamb at one time or another: rejected, passed over, laughed at, or looked down on.

That's because, much like the bummer lamb, the weak and needy in this world are often pushed to the background, while the strong are applauded and admired. Wherever we may fall on the spectrum, we constantly compare ourselves with one another, believing our value is determined by how we measure up to others.

We fool ourselves if we think we're immune to comparison as Christians. In fact, we often take it a step further: We measure our worth to God using the world's value system.

If we're successful, God must be smiling down on us because we're clearly doing something right. If we're weak, sick, or struggling, God must be disappointed in us because we're clearly of no use to him in that state or, worse, we're being punished for something we must have done.

But this faulty framework never leads us to the heart of God. It only props us up in pride or plunges us down in shame. Even Jesus's closest friends found themselves stumbling into these pitfalls time and time again.

The good news is, God's value system offers freedom from striving for acceptance and worth by our own merit. But first, we have to know what that value system is.

GOD'S VALUE SYSTEM

Luke 9:46–48 gives us a bird's-eye view of how God defines value and greatness:

> An argument arose among them as to which of them was the greatest. But Jesus, knowing the reasoning of their hearts, took a child and put him by his side and said to them, "Whoever receives this child in my name receives me, and whoever receives me receives him who sent me. For he who is least among you all is the one who is great."

In this passage, the disciples argued over who was the greatest. It was a pretty bold question to ask Jesus. If I had been observing this interaction, I would have cringed, anxiously awaiting Jesus's rebuke. But his response was unsurprised and calm. He presented them with a new framework for what true greatness is in God's eyes.

For he who is least among you all is the one who is great.

The visual he chose was a child who had no impressive résumé, no money to his name, and no great acts of righteousness to use in bargaining for Jesus's love and acceptance. And that's a theme we'll see all throughout the Gospels—Jesus calling people to himself with nothing to bring but childlike faith.

To see why, let's look ahead a bit to 1 Corinthians 1:27–29, where God flips the world's value system even more on its head:

> God chose what is foolish in the world to shame the wise; God chose what is weak in the world to shame the strong; God chose what is low and despised in the world, even things that are not, to bring to nothing things that are, so that no human being might boast in the presence of God.

Consider the motley crew Jesus chose to be his disciples. Several were lowly fishermen, one was a Zealot attempting to overthrow the Roman government, and another was a despised tax collector. Jesus could have chosen disciples from among the impressive religious leaders, those powerful in the government, or the wealthy to fund his ministry, but he didn't. He sought out the least impressive of society.

Why?

Because it's the poor, needy, despised, and lowly of society who are truly awake to their great need. Those aware of their unworthiness knew they had nothing to bring to Jesus but everything to gain by trusting him. So by calling disciples who weren't strong and impressive, he could display his strength and glory.

And the same is true for you.

RETHINKING GREATNESS

Greatness in the world's eyes is measured by what we can do for ourselves. Greatness in God's eyes is measured by taking our eyes *off ourselves* and trusting in him.

Throughout Scripture we see how comfort and success are a greater threat to our souls than pain and limitation. Success subtly tells us the lie that we're self-sufficient beings. Little by little, we stop feeling the need for wisdom or help outside ourselves. We wouldn't necessarily say it out loud, but at times, we're kind of impressed with ourselves. Or at the very least, we work hard to impress those around us.

Not only is this exhausting, but we're also in danger of forgetting that everything we have comes from the hand of God—including our talents, opportunities, and the results of our efforts. This is why we're warned in Mark 8:36, "What good is it for someone to gain the whole world, yet forfeit their soul?" (NIV).

Struggle, on the other hand, may feel like a sign of God's disapproval, but it may be his loving protection to keep us dependent on him. According to the world's metrics, failure looks like our downfall. But from the Lord's perspective, challenges that keep us near to the heart of Jesus are a far greater blessing than temporary success.

An ankle injury in high school that put a sudden end to my plans to play Division 1 basketball robbed me of so much I desired—taking a piece of my earthly identity with it. Years later, I can now see how God allowed me to lose something good in order to give me something greater. The pain and loss I experienced were what he used to redirect the course of my life, ultimately showing me that my true identity was in him, not in the accolades or successes of this world.

Think back to the bummer lamb analogy for a moment. A person who achieves earthly greatness may look like the fattest of the flock, contently gorging himself on the lushest grass without a care in the world. All the while, a wolf is lying in wait as the most admired sheep proudly meanders farther and farther away from the shepherd. His confident self-sufficiency, full stomach, and false sense of security may look impressive to the rest of the flock, but in reality, he's in the greatest danger because he strayed from the wisdom and protection of the shepherd.

On the other hand, the bummer lamb may look like a disappointment, unimpressive to those around him. But his sense of need may very well be what will keep him close to the provision and protection of the one watching over him. The bummer lamb's shortcomings may tempt him to believe he's less valuable than the stronger sheep in the flock. However, the bummer is the most secure because he's covered and cared for by the shepherd, who not only knows him by name but is also willing to lay down his own life to save his lamb.

JESUS DRAWS NEAR TO THE LEAST OF THESE

Even if someone is vaguely impressed by something I have to offer, deep down I know the weaknesses and struggles within. You know those people who can keep an immaculate house at all times so they're never embarrassed when someone shows up unexpectedly? Yeah, that's not me. You know those people who are so savvy and charismatic that they can sell sand to people on the beach? That's not me either. You know those people who religiously wake up to run ten miles, rain or shine? Nope, not a chance. I'm more likely to sarcastically quote the verse "The wicked run when no one is chasing them" (Proverbs 28:1, GNT) than I am to lace up my running shoes at five in the morning.

I'm a washed-up athlete who can no longer do much of what I enjoy after my devastating injury. I'm a mom who's been stretched and challenged far beyond what I ever imagined possible. I can't keep a plant alive for the life of me. If you tell me your name, I'll forget it two seconds later, and I'm living in a body that's technically alive but sick enough to keep me from truly living. In many ways, I'm a bummer lamb.

And yet, after years of despising my lowliness, I can honestly say I'm thankful, because the very things that bring me low nudge me nearer to the heart of Jesus. He's my Shepherd who loves me, not because I'm impressive, but because I'm his.

That's why I love the interactions Jesus had with people of all walks of life during his time on earth. His heart was clearly drawn to the least of these. He got down to the level of little children with tenderness and affection. He drew near to the sick, lame, and demon-possessed, laying his healing hands on them when society saw them as repulsive, disposable, and hopeless. He pursued the sinner who hung their head in shame, offering their weary soul hope and new life in his forgiveness. And the risen Jesus chose to reveal himself to women before anyone else on the day of his resurrection, despite a culture that viewed them as unreliable and inferior to men.

Jesus drew near to the lowly then, and he draws near to the lowly now. Our great Shepherd rescues us in our helpless state, beckoning us to surrender our self-reliant ways and sinful hearts to find peace, joy, rest, and safety in his unfailing love.

We may very well be bummer lambs in the world's eyes, but as God proves through his relentless pursuit of us, we are treasured lambs in the eyes of our Shepherd.

Do you hear his voice? He's calling you by name.

Meeting with Jesus

1. In what ways can you relate to the bummer lamb? In what ways have you believed the world's version of greatness over God's?
2. What have your weaknesses, failures, or sins led you to feel about yourself compared with those around you? Read 1 Corinthians 1:27–29. Journal how these verses show God's view of your weaknesses.
3. In what ways are you pursuing earthly success over knowing Jesus and being made more like him? Ask God to reveal those areas to you, and write down any practical changes he's inviting you to make.

PART 2

FEAR AND SHAME

6

When Change Feels Impossible

Luke 4:1–15

"I just don't know how to react any other way."

Some close friends and I were talking through struggles of marriage and motherhood, one of them being sinful anger and yelling. One friend admitted her impulse to bark back in anger at her kids. She confessed how habitual this response had become for her, how easy and natural it felt to speak harshly, and how hard it seemed to do anything different. All of us understood.

Sin habits die hard—so hard that we don't even think to fight them anymore, because we aren't convinced we can. In our hearts we believe the lie *I just can't change.*

This may be one of our enemy's most original lies. From the beginning sin has been crouching at our door (Genesis 4:7), and we're so quick to give it entrance. Maybe we believe sin isn't *that* bad. Or maybe we see its seriousness but it feels too hard to do anything about it. Either way, we know what it's like to be duped by sin and shamed by its consequences—and to wonder if change is even possible for us.

Is change possible? If so, how?

TEMPTED . . . AS WE ARE?

Beyond the staggering reality that the Lord Jesus was fully human on earth—walking around on two legs, getting hungry and thirsty, laughing and crying, and needing sleep after a long day—now we turn to the reality that he was also tempted. Take this in: The Son of God experienced temptation, just like you do. But how, exactly?

If you're like me, the idea that Jesus was tempted is a mental wrestle. "Jesus, the superhero" card gets pulled in your head. *Wait*, you think. *Since Jesus is the Son of God—fully divine and fully human—how could he be tempted like I am? Doesn't his perfect, sinless self mean he actually doesn't get what I'm going through? Isn't he too good to understand my temptations?*

Like a superhero's strength that far surpasses a mere mortal's, Jesus's divine nature makes us . . . skeptical. We wonder if he *really* understands what we face. The blood-boiling anger we feel toward our kids. Our attraction to a certain person (or image) that isn't our spouse. The ever-increasing desire for pleasure or power. Does Jesus really get us in *these* places of our hearts?

Yes. Jesus actually knows every facet and force of temptation you will ever face, to its full extent. He exhausted it all because, unlike us, he was able to resist every last bit of it. Hebrews 4:15 is entirely true of Jesus: "We do not have a high priest who is unable to sympathize with our weaknesses, but one who *in every respect* has been tempted as we are, yet without sin."

Each of us faces temptation—the enticement to do wrong—but we don't always give in to it. Sometimes we fight well. Other times we fight . . . for a while. Because our hearts are fallen, however, we don't usually get very far in our fight, yielding more quickly to temptation than we would like. But Jesus never yielded. He never caved or gave in. He knows the full strength of temptation because he resisted it in full.

But then there's the "yet without sin" part. It's a great comfort to us that Jesus fully knows our temptations, but since he *wasn't* a sinner, how could he know exactly what we endure?

Think about it: Jesus's holiness meant his temptations were *more* grievous to encounter, not less. This might be hard for us to grasp, because we are so far from holy. A child simply doesn't know what their parents face as fully grown adults who are much more mature than they are. Parents feel the full weight of responsibility. Similarly, as the holy Son of God, "Jesus felt the force of temptation more than we can imagine. Sinlessness heightens, not lessens, temptation."[1]

Knowing these two realities—that Jesus exhausted every temptation and did so with excruciating, holy grief in his heart—we now turn to Luke's account of Jesus in the wilderness.

TWO TRUTHS ABOUT TEMPTATION

You know that gnawing feeling of hunger that's accompanied by a lack of self-control? In our house, we call that being "hangry." Can you imagine how Jesus felt after not eating for more than a month? "Hungry" is an understatement. But that's how Luke describes him as he sets the scene: "Jesus, full of the Holy Spirit, returned from the Jordan and was led by the Spirit in the wilderness for forty days, being tempted by the devil. And he ate nothing during those days. And when they were ended, he was hungry" (Luke 4:1–2).

No doubt Jesus was (and is) fully human.

In chapter 2, we learned that Jesus is the second Adam. Adam's sin devastated our humanity, but the sinlessness of Jesus heals us. Adam was tempted by the devil, and he failed. Now we see Jesus being tempted by the same devil, who uses the same tactics as he did in the garden. The scene is painted all over again. What will the outcome be?

The connection to Adam here is also a connection to you and me. *Every believer will enter into temptation.* If Adam did—if *Jesus* did—

why wouldn't we? It seems obvious. But we're so often caught off guard by temptation, surprised by its presence, lured by its power, and then frustrated that we gave in, again. Peter's words are a needed reminder: "Beloved, do not be surprised at the fiery trial when it comes upon you to test you, as though something strange were happening to you" (1 Peter 4:12). Temptation isn't strange or surprising. It's normal and expected. This means we can walk through today with eyes wide open. Jesus's encouragement to his disciples goes for us too: "Watch and pray that you may not enter into temptation. The spirit indeed is willing, but the flesh is weak" (Matthew 26:41).

Here's a second (very encouraging) truth from Luke's account: *Believers never enter into temptation apart from the presence of the Holy Spirit*. Who accompanied Jesus in the wilderness? Who, in fact, *led* him there (Luke 4:1)? It was God's Spirit, who came on him in full measure at his baptism (Matthew 3:16; Mark 1:10; Luke 3:22; John 1:32–34). And the same Spirit who led and empowered Jesus will also lead and empower us:

> Walk by the Spirit, and you will not gratify the desires of the flesh. . . . If you are led by the Spirit, you are not under the law. . . . The fruit of the Spirit is love, joy, peace, patience, kindness, goodness, faithfulness, gentleness, self-control; against such things there is no law. . . .
>
> If we live by the Spirit, let us also keep in step with the Spirit. (Galatians 5:16, 18, 22–23, 25)

Satan came to Jesus in a time of bodily weakness and tempted him in ways he often tempts us: immediate gratification, identity, power, and devotion. Where do we seek our satisfaction or sense of purpose? Where do we turn for companionship, peace, pleasure, or happiness? We will be most tempted in these areas to turn from full reliance on God's Spirit to a temporary god, especially if that god is ourselves. Yet Luke reminds us very simply but very reassuringly that *we already have what we seek*—the all-sufficient God with and within us. We are not alone.

And we can indeed change, even little by little.

If you belong to Christ, you have his Spirit (Romans 8:9–10).

And if you have his Spirit, you have everything you need to face temptation and fight your sin.

ONE MORE ALL-IMPORTANT TRUTH

Okay, great, you think. *This sounds nice in theory, but Jesus was perfect, and I'm not. I don't always listen to the Spirit. What then?* You and me both, my friend. I woke up today and prayed that God would help me be patient and gentle with my family—and I blew it about five minutes later. (Cue the tears.) Fighting temptation can feel so discouraging. We need a kind of encouragement beyond the "you've got this" mantras our world tosses around. We need truth that runs deeper even than the "God's got this" clichés that Christians toss around.

We need a perfect person to live in our place.

Jesus is this person.

As we read about how the Son of God faced his enemy, we notice several things: An unyielding allegiance to his Father's will. An obedient commitment to his Father's commands. A strengthening vision of his Father's glory.

Everything we haven't done and everything we most need.

Jesus's sinless record, his perfect and unmatched goodness in the face of evil, is our only hope. At the end of the day—even our very best day with no obvious sin or failures—we are unholy compared with our spotless, holy God. We have no arguments before him. We can't stand beside him. We are not him.

He alone is holy, and we are absolutely, positively not.

So it's a good thing that Jesus lives (and loves) to change sinful people like us (Hebrews 7:25).

Christ was the only man who never yielded to temptation, and he did it for us. He did this so his perfect and sinless record before God could be given to us, covering us and all our sin. When we are united to him by faith, Jesus's victory in the wilderness becomes our victory. His obedience becomes our obedience. His allegiance becomes ours, too, and so does his very Spirit. Not only does his Spirit grant these blessings to us; he also generates them through us. *Now* we can have victory over temptation. *Now* we can obey. *Now* we desire to bow to God and give him glory.

Now we can actually change.

OUR SYMPATHETIC, STRENGTHENING PRIEST

Friend, Jesus was tempted like you in every way on earth, and now he is the perfect person to sustain you in every way from heaven. He meets you right here in your place of need, praying for you, just like he did for Peter: "Simon, Simon, behold, Satan demanded to have you, that he might sift you like wheat, but I have prayed for you that your faith may not fail" (Luke 22:31–32). Peter entered into temptation and blew it, denying his Savior three times, but the enemy didn't win, because Peter's faith didn't fail. He returned to the Savior he loved, and he was forgiven and commissioned for a Spirit-led life of obedience and costly sacrifice (verse 32; John 21:15–19).*

Do you need to return to your Lord today? Or is he calling you to come for the first time? His arms are open. His heart is tender toward your temptations and full of grace to forgive you. He promises mercy and help in your time of need because he *knows* your need (Hebrews 4:16).

He fought to the end, and now you can too.

---

* More on this in chapter 19.

Meeting with Jesus

1. Read Luke 4:1–15. Which of Jesus's temptations do you most identify with? Why? It's wise to get clear on exactly what battles you are fighting so you can bring them to God.
2. After reading this chapter, how would you describe Jesus's ability to understand your temptations?
3. Journal some ways you need the Holy Spirit's strength and help today, and write a prayer asking him to empower you for a holy walk with Jesus.

7

When You Want to Hide

John 4:1–42

I rolled over in bed, my lips sealed shut by pride. What a drastic turn the day had taken—and it was my fault. My husband and I had gone from laughing together after a sweet day as a family to turning away from each other as we murmured good night. And it was all because I hadn't weighed my words. I had spoken rashly to him, assuming the worst about a comment he made and then shutting down the conversation when we should've resolved it. As I lay there in the dark, my heart was heavy with conviction—but not heavy enough to do something about it. Not yet at least.

I'm not the only one to hide in response to sin and shame. Remember what happened to Adam? After he and his wife ate the forbidden fruit, they couldn't get away from God fast enough. Genesis 3 tells us Adam's reason: "I heard the sound of you in the garden, and I was afraid, because I was naked, and I hid myself" (verse 10). Why did he hide? Because he was scared, for two related reasons: God is holy and perfect, and he was no longer like God.

Adam had become altogether different from his Creator, and he knew it.

We know it, too, don't we? We know the desperate, sinking unease we feel when we've wronged someone we really love. We know the piercing clarity of conviction after we've gone down the wrong path. We know the shame and embarrassment we feel when we've blown it. We know what Adam felt that day in Eden.

The Samaritan woman knew what he felt too.

SIN IS OUR BIGGEST PROBLEM

When John sets the scene for us, we're told that Jesus and his disciples had been traveling on foot, "and he had to pass through Samaria" (John 4:4). In Jewish eyes, Samaritans were religious outcasts. They were impure half breeds, the descendants of Jews who had intermarried with foreigners after the Assyrian conquest. So John bluntly tells us, "Jews have no dealings with Samaritans" (verse 9). But not this Jew—not Jesus. Jesus is unconcerned about appearances and status. He cares about our hearts, not our history. He is ready and willing to receive anyone who will come to him—even a Samaritan and even a woman.[1] Even very sinful people like us.

Let's think for a moment about this word *sin*.

It's an uncomfortable church word that many people don't like. But it's also a biblical word, a reality that God refuses to sugarcoat and calls out in love. Far more than the most intentional parents who train their kids for their good, our heavenly Father wants us to see the truth about ourselves. Sin is an offense against him, the Holy One, the opposite of his very nature, and it means the difference between eternal life and eternal death for us. It was Adam's sin that made him want to hide from God. Why? Because God's holiness was no longer a comfort. It was now like a piercing spotlight on Adam's unholiness.

Unless we look our sin in the face and call it what it is, we fool ourselves.

But we can't fool God.

Just as Jesus knew the Samaritan woman's every sinful choice (which we'll see in a moment), he knows everything about you. Nothing can be hidden from him (Psalm 139:1–6), because he is the all-knowing God. And that's a good thing. A disease can't be cured unless it's first diagnosed, and God's Word tells us that our sin is like a disease (Jeremiah 17:9). It's the greatest problem of our humanity, and it's killing us. It's also keeping us from the freedom and joy God has in store for all his people. What is a holy God to do?

He draws near to do something about it.

JESUS IS DRAWN TO SINNERS

Don't miss what John says first about Jesus: "Wearied as he was from his journey, [he] was sitting beside [Jacob's] well" (John 4:6). Once again, we're struck by Jesus's utter humanity. The Son of God was weary—tired from traveling and preaching—and he was also thirsty (verse 7). His human need for a rest and a drink of water encourages us, as J. C. Ryle says, to draw near to him who understands us:

> When we cry to Him in the hour of bodily pain and weakness, He knows well what we mean. When our prayers and praises are feeble through bodily weariness, He can understand our condition. He knows our frame. He has learned by experience what it is to be a man.[2]

So Jesus gets my physical condition, we think, *but what about my sin?* We wonder how the perfect, sinless Son of God can relate to our biggest problem, which he doesn't share. Doesn't our sin repulse him? Doesn't it offend him and make us want to shrink back in shame, like Adam did in the garden?

It is true that our sin offends our holy God. But because of Jesus visiting us in the flesh, now we can approach God in a whole new way. Lest we think that Jesus's holiness makes him unapproachable, it actually does the opposite: His sinless compassion makes him most able to comfort sinners.

When the Samaritan woman approached the well, she came at high noon, the most sweltering time of day. She was avoiding the crowds. But just when she thought she was well hidden, she was most exposed and ran into Jesus, the searcher of every heart. This Jewish man wasn't offended by her at all, and in an act of humility he started the conversation: "Give me a drink" (verse 7).

Isn't this how Jesus approaches us? When we, too, have tried to carefully avoid him, even outright dismissing him and going our own way, when our greed and lust and selfishness and pride seem more pleasurable than the Glorious One, when our repeated sin patterns have worn us down with discouragement, when we feel too far gone for anyone's forgiveness or love, Jesus draws near to us.

Notice how he spoke to catch the woman's attention. He's speaking to catch *your* attention, too, and he does this by waiting for you in Scripture.

He offers himself to you—the sinful you, the untidy you, the real you.

The Samaritan woman's encounter with Jesus is good news because it means you don't need to clean yourself up before coming to him. You can't, actually. The enemy will lie to you that you need to, and your own heart will tell you that you can. But sin's disease makes this impossible, and *this* is why Jesus came to you first. The woman asked, "How is it that you, a Jew, ask for a drink from *me*?" (verse 9). Jesus responded with an invitation:

> If you knew the gift of God, and who it is that is saying to you, "Give me a drink," you would have asked him, and he would have given you living water. . . . The water that I will give [you] will become in [you] a spring of water welling up to eternal life. (verses 10, 14)

Don't you love how Jesus used pictures to make his point? We need water. Human thirst never ends. Every day, our bodies need proper hydration to survive and thrive. And even if I drink tons of water today, I will still need more of it tomorrow. Can you fathom never needing to refill your cup, because your body has a built-in water source? Imagine never being thirsty again and *always* feeling satisfied.

One of the reasons we choose to sin is that we're seeking satisfaction in the wrong places, in "broken cisterns" that can never quench our spiritual thirst, because they "can hold no water" (Jeremiah 2:13). Sin is a terrible fountain, a poisonous and leaky well, that only makes us thirstier and eventually kills us. But Jesus's water? It's a never-ending spring of satisfaction, peace, and joy, one he invites us to draw our deepest needs from now and every day, into eternity (Isaiah 12:3).

And to draw from the well of salvation, we must start with conviction of sin.

JESUS IS THE REMEDY FOR SINNERS

"Sir, give me this water," the woman said (John 4:15). She wanted what Jesus had to offer, even if she didn't fully get what he meant. This man was different, she could tell. But how different, she was about to see. Jesus offered her his living water by exposing her need: "Go, call your husband, and come here" (verse 16). The woman had been called out, and she knew it.

When Jesus draws near to us, he doesn't pretend everything is okay. That would be a lie, and our God can't lie (Titus 1:2). Remember, a disease can't be cured unless it's first diagnosed, and that's what Jesus does. He exposed the woman's shady history of failed marriages and, in all likelihood, adultery, and he did so to heal her. Ryle says, "The first draught of living water which our Lord gave to the Samaritan woman was conviction of sin. . . . No one values the physician until he feels his disease."[3]

What sin is the Holy Spirit calling out in you right now?

He does it to heal you. He reveals it in his gracious mercy.

He won't crush you with it but promises to overwhelm you with the life-giving, sin-cleansing waters of his love. His cure begins with conviction of sin, of anything that would keep you from Jesus, for no true life can be found apart from him.

Repentance is the invitation that opens the door to fellowship with God.

There's another big church word: *repentance.* It sounds complicated, but it's quite simple. To repent means to turn away from your sin and toward Christ. It's a shift in direction. It's an attitude of the heart that says no to sin and yes to God, no to the life-suppressing disease and yes to the cure. When Jesus called out the woman's five husbands and her current boyfriend (John 4:17–18), he was inviting her to repent. He says, *There is no need to hide, because you can't anyway. Instead, turn to me. I have what you most desire and need.*

The word *repentance* can make us squirm. Why? Because it requires submission. A letting go of control. A giving up of momentary pleasure. A surrendering of the lie that we're the god of our own life. If we're honest, we'd rather distract ourselves from having to think about sin, even if that means sinning more. But surrendering to an enemy isn't the same thing as submitting to a friend or a good authority. One intends to enslave us; the other fights for us. Instead of seeing repentance as losing ourselves, we need to reframe it as finding the much greater good that God has for us.

When Jesus confronts our sin, he doesn't leave us sitting in it.

He leads us to himself. To his forgiveness and to a new life of devotion to him.

At its heart, sin is a worship issue—an issue of our devotion. When we sin, what we're saying is "I love _____ more than I love the Lord." I love my own agenda more than I love God's will, so I will control people and vent my anger even if it hurts them and me.

I love being honored by others more than I love God's opinion, so I will do whatever it takes to please people. Or in the woman's case, I love being loved—even if only temporarily—more than I love resting in God's love for me. Misdirected devotion leads to sin and shame. But Jesus sets us free to devote ourselves to God.

"The Father is seeking such people to worship him" (verse 23).

Now, this certainly doesn't mean perfection. If you, dear reader, have already turned to Jesus, you know how sin can die hard. But repentance isn't a one-and-done act. It's ongoing—day by day, moment by moment, as we turn again to Jesus in faith that he will forgive us, cleanse us, and strengthen us for another day.

Do you hear the invitation? God seeks you right now through his Son, who waits for you, speaks to you in his Word, and meets you there. No matter who you are, where you've been, or what you've done, Jesus seeks *you*. So, yes, you have a great big problem. So do I. But Jesus is a greater Savior. He's the one person who fully understands the battle against sin, who loves broken, sinful people—enough to sit beside a well and ask a hurting woman for a drink, then take her into his very heart. Because he is also God.

The heart of the person before us makes all the difference. If I had realized my husband's desire to forgive and support me, I wouldn't have waited until the next morning to apologize. Christ confronts you in order to heal you, friend, if you will only give him your heart—sin, shame, and all.

So the next time you give in to misdirected worship and lesser loves, remember your Father seeks you. You can approach him through Jesus. There's no need to hide; in fact, you can't anyway. Instead, you can submit to him, for he seeks you not to condemn you but to set you free from sin.

And "out of [your] heart will flow rivers of living water" (John 7:38).

Meeting with Jesus

1. Are you afraid to be honest with God about your struggles? If so, how does John 4:1–42 encourage you to bring yourself to him in complete honesty?
2. Do you feel shame when you've done something wrong, or do you prefer to avoid thinking about it altogether? What do you think you're running from?
3. Read 1 John 1:9. Share with the Lord the temptations you're facing and the sins you're battling right now.

8

When Fear Consumes You

Mark 4:37–40

I'm going to shoot straight with you here. I write on the topic of fear not because I have it figured out but because it's still a battle. Fear isn't something you conquer once and never give way to again. It's a lifelong training ground, where I'm standing right alongside you as I face countless health, financial, parental, and other unknowns. Most acutely right now, I'm battling deep, sick-to-my-stomach dread over an extremely difficult health journey ahead. The likelihood is that things will get far worse before they get better. In my weary body, any pain beyond what I already endure sounds not only unbearable but also terrifying.

Needless to say, there's a lot to fear in this world. Invisible germs lie in wait to ruin our long-awaited plans. Economies crash. Natural disasters wipe away lives and earthly treasures in a matter of minutes. Decay and death come to all—often when we least expect them.

Whether we like to admit it or not, when the inevitable storms of life rock us, we're all faced with the unsettling reality of how little we can control. And when we feel out of control, fear lies in wait and what-ifs consume us.

Can you relate? Whether it's little nagging fears in the background or bigger ones that cripple, I'm sure you can quickly pinpoint the gnawing worries that threaten your peace right now.

But the good news is this: Jesus knows your fear. Not as a spectator from the shoreline, but as a strong Savior standing with you in the midst of it. Even more, he can do something about it—just like he did when his disciples cried out in panic as the stormy sea threatened to consume them.

AFRAID IN THE STORM

As we've already seen in previous chapters, Jesus empathizes with us because he's been there. He trembled at the horrors of the cross, and he also endured with his disciples when fear dissolved their faith.

He wasn't surprised by it then, and he isn't surprised by it now. So he doesn't scold us for our gut reaction of fear but encourages us to bring our fretful selves to him in faith that he is wise enough and strong enough to handle what we can't. He knows that fear will tempt us toward unbelief, but he also knows that faith can put fear in its proper place.

In the gospel of Mark, that's precisely what he taught the disciples when a storm threatened their safety. The disciples climbed aboard a boat to sail across the lake with Jesus. Suddenly . . .

> A great windstorm arose, and the waves were breaking over the boat, so that the boat was already being swamped. [Jesus] was in the stern, sleeping on the cushion. So they woke him up and said to him, "Teacher! Don't you care that we're going to die?"
>
> He got up, rebuked the wind, and said to the sea, "Silence! Be still!" The wind ceased, and there was a

> great calm. Then he said to them, "Why are you afraid? Do you still have no faith?" (4:37–40, CSB)

This passage is chock-full of practical takeaways for us.

1. We Don't Endure Storms Alone

Fear and doubt lie to us that if Jesus really loved us, he'd protect us from anything bad. Personally, despite all the hardships I've endured, I still naturally assume God's blessing and favor will come wrapped in the form of an easier life. That's because we expect heaven now, despite living in a fallen world. The truth is, just because God is in control and promises to redeem all things doesn't mean the natural world is free from the curse of sin—or the pain it brings with it. Disasters still happen, disease still haunts, and evil still seems to win. Although God never delights in our suffering, it is a natural part of sin's consequences, and we won't be free from it until Jesus returns.

If that were all there were to it, we'd have every reason to fear. But because Jesus made a way to free us from sin's eternal consequences through his sacrifice, we can be saved from our greatest fear of all. Now God takes what sin meant to destroy and redeems these fear-inducing circumstances to lead us to a life-giving faith in him that casts out fear. In the paradox of faith, we sometimes come to find that the greatest, most lasting blessings of all come wrapped in the least desirable packages.

In his divinity, Jesus knew the storm would arise. But he got into the boat with the disciples anyway. In the same way, he knows the trials that will come to you. He doesn't pat you on the back, send you out into life's storms, and yell, "You've got this!" No, he gets into the boat with you. He's committed to enduring every moment of them alongside you, and his comfort and power are at your disposal (Isaiah 43:2).

2. Jesus May Seem Asleep, but He's Still in Control

Like the disciples, I've often felt battered by a terrifying storm while Jesus appears blissfully asleep. As if I'm playing a game of Marco Polo in tumultuous waters, I call out, "Jesus! Are you there? Why are you silent? Don't you see the waves threatening to sink me?" Sometimes his silence is an absolute mystery I can't make sense of at the moment. And there's a reason for that. God said plainly in Isaiah 55:8–9,

> My thoughts are not your thoughts,
> neither are your ways my ways, declares the LORD.
> For as the heavens are higher than the earth,
> so are my ways higher than your ways
> and my thoughts than your thoughts.

God calls us to trust *who* he says he is—good, faithful, and trustworthy—rather than *what* we can make sense of. To the disciples, Jesus looked unaware of and indifferent to their plight. To us, he can seem distant and silent. But we can't miss the spiritual analogy when Mark tells us how "[Jesus] was in the stern, sleeping on the cushion" (Mark 4:38, CSB). Jesus may have been resting in his physically weary body, but he was still in the stern of the boat—where the direction of the vessel is controlled.

The disciples feared and panicked, but Jesus was ultimately in control. He was so at peace in his Father's sovereignty that he was able to rest in the midst of a storm. He knew he was secure in his Father's will.

Thankfully, the same is true for us. If God is good and his plan is trustworthy, we can truly rest in him rather than fearfully trying to control things. The more we release the fear of what we can't control, the more we can rest in Jesus's presence and trust his control over all that happens.

3. Even a Little Faith Is Enough

The disciples' words of accusation sadly echo my own response at times: "Teacher! Don't you care that we're going to die?" (Mark 4:38, CSB). They weren't just questioning the Son of God's power; they were questioning his character. Even though they had seen him perform miracles, at the first sign of danger, their gut reaction was to question his love for them.

It's easy to criticize the disciples, thinking we would have responded differently. But this temptation is all too familiar—even for followers of Jesus who have the full Word of God and his Holy Spirit within us. When fear rears its ugly head, we're just as tempted to give way to unbelief. We buy into the enemy's lies:

God doesn't care.
God isn't able.
Of course this would happen to you.
You'd be better off on your own.
Your circumstances are hopeless.
You could never survive if that happened to you.
If God loved you, he'd protect you from this.
Hard circumstances are a threat to your happiness.

I know the inner fear dialogue well.

Before we beat ourselves up, let's be encouraged by Jesus's heart for us in this place: He doesn't reject us. And he doesn't require a perfect faith to hear and answer our prayers. On the surface, the disciples' words sound like a faithless accusation; however, underneath there was, in fact, a small kernel of faith. They didn't try to save themselves. Instead, they cried out to Jesus—however imperfectly.

God doesn't require perfect faith to hear and answer our cries.

He immediately responded when they turned to him in dependence, even though their words were filled with doubt, fear, and confusion. And we, too, can cry out honestly, even if we feel like we're treading water in the tumultuous waves of uncertainty.

GRUMBLING VERSUS GROANING

What makes the difference? We can either cry out *against* Jesus or cry out *to* him. Grumbling about him is a sin of unbelief that enforces doubt and fear. But when we humbly go to him with our questions and fears, he draws near with compassion. A broken and contrite heart he will not despise—even if our faith feels weak and vulnerable (Psalm 51:17).

Jesus mercifully calmed the wind and the waves, despite the disciples' weak faith. His response wasn't dependent on the strength of their faith; it was dependent on *his* faithfulness.

But now we have to face the massive elephant in the room, don't we? Sometimes God chooses *not* to change our circumstances. Although Jesus immediately calmed the storm, we've all experienced times when God chose not to calm ours when we desperately wanted him to. Often he simply doesn't give us answers as to why he heals one person's sickness and not another's or why he sometimes brings immediate relief and other times calls us to long-suffering.

What we can't forget is this: Our earthly challenges are temporary, but who we are—our character, faith, and souls—is eternal. Sometimes God's love is shown through removing a trial, and even then, he intends to grow us at a heart level. Often, however, lasting growth comes only as he equips us to endure the storm, rather than sparing us from it.

Think about it. If God always protected us or immediately removed trials, would we ever learn to trust him? Likely not. He knows that our hearts are bent toward independence, self-reliance, and control and that we're drawn toward immediate gratification rather than lasting satisfaction. He loves us enough to, at times, delay the relief we desire, because he has something greater in store for us. He wants more for us than being helplessly tossed by the wind and waves. So in his kindness, he allows that which will stretch our faith and keep us near to him—both now and when new storms arise.

But his love for us also means he won't allow one gust of wind beyond what he will redeem for our good. Just as he commanded the wind to cease, he sets the boundaries to our storms.

Friend, it's false comfort to believe God will prevent our fears from becoming reality. Not because he can't, but because he hasn't promised it. We can, however, find comfort in rehearsing the truth that he will meet us with his grace regardless of what lies ahead. Our peace is found not in the promise of no pain but in knowing we'll have the presence of Jesus when it comes.

Vaneetha Risner writes, "Replacing 'what if' with 'even if' is one of the most liberating exchanges we can ever make. We trade our irrational fears of an uncertain future for the loving assurance of an unchanging God. We see that even if the worst happens, God will carry us."[1]

What are you afraid of right now? Remember, what-if borrows tomorrow's problems before we've been given the grace to endure them. When worry whispers that you're at the mercy of chance, fight back with the truth that you are secure in the hands of a merciful God. He may allow what doesn't feel good in the moment, but he is with you, ready to meet you with everything you need until the sun breaks through the clouds.

Today, if you feel weak in faith and weary of crying out, don't lose hope. God isn't disappointed by your battle against fear, because as your Great High Priest, he's been there. He hasn't left you to fend for yourself.

Think of the worries and fears that are taking up residence in your mind right now. Stop for a moment and read Matthew 26:36–44, specifically looking at how Jesus responded to the horrors he would face in his death.

The Bible shows us that when Jesus was greatly troubled in the garden, he fell face down and prayed for God to remove the cross from his future. In his humanity, it was impossible to bear. But then he turned his eyes to his Father, whom he trusted above all else. He gave God the power that fear had over him and received his Father's power to endure whatever lay ahead in his strength.

If you feel tossed by the waves of life and wonder if Jesus cares, be encouraged by his heart for you: He endured in his Father's strength what no one else could so that he can now give you all you need to endure in his. If you fear the future, remember his grace is sufficient for *today*. Whatever the future holds, his grace will meet you there.

Meeting with Jesus

1. In what ways are you tempted to live by fear? Which fears stem from current circumstances, and which stem from future circumstances you have curated within your own mind?
2. Read Psalm 34:4. What do you think the psalmist means when he writes, "[God] delivered me from all my fears"? Do you think that means that God removed or prevented the circumstances he feared or that God delivered him from the *fear* of those circumstances?
3. What characteristics of Jesus are seen through his interaction with the disciples on the boat? How do those characteristics comfort you in your fears? Come to him honestly today and ask for his help to rest in the promise of his presence, rather than living in fear of what you can't control.

9

When You Wonder What God *Really* Thinks of You

Matthew 18:1–14

"What is *wrong* with you?" The words fly out of my mouth before I can stop them, and they sting. My child looks at me with teary eyes because I have just confirmed one of their worst nightmares: Something is very, very wrong with them, and their mom has had enough.

At the end of everything, the fear of rejection haunts us all. We're well aware that, deep down, something is wrong with us. And that's the hard truth. Sin has made everything terribly wrong, as much as we pretend it isn't so. You know it and I know it. But true as this may be and guilty as we are, sin has also told us terrible lies about our God.

We have come to believe he has had quite enough of us.

Isn't there a limit? we wonder. *Doesn't God get tired of me and the sins I keep falling into?* We are realists. We know how frustrating it is when people keep failing us, so isn't God just as frustrated as we are, if not more? We picture God wringing his hands and shaking his head as he blurts out, "What is *wrong* with you?"

At the core of all our questions is a very important one: *What does God really think about me?* Much of our Christian walk involves reorientation about who God is and how he deals with us.[1] We are creatures made in his image who have gravely marred that image, so our beliefs often need correcting. Have you ever considered how you project onto God your own thoughts about yourself, others, and the world around you? Sin's corrupting power has altered the way we think about him. Now we suspect him rather than trust him. Now we blame him rather than yield to him. And since other peoples' sin and failures frustrate us and cause us to abandon ship, we assume God feels the same way.

This is why we so badly need his Word.

What does God actually think about us? Let's turn to Matthew 18 for three answers to this question.

GOD THINKS YOUR NEEDINESS IS BEAUTIFUL

"Who is the greatest in the kingdom of heaven?" (Matthew 18:1). The disciples asked Jesus about status, and they proved what we just admitted: We so often project onto God what we think. But Jesus flips our earthly reasoning upside down: "Truly, I say to you, *unless you turn and become like children,* you will never enter the kingdom of heaven" (verse 3).

Become like children? Does God think greatness is attained by . . . littleness? As we've seen, this idea runs counter to everything we believe about our value. Ladder climbing and elbow throwing are the human way. Those are natural for us. But they're not Jesus's way.

God thinks needy children are beautiful, praiseworthy, *great.*

So what are little children like? If you have kids or if you've spent any amount of time around them, you know how needy, needy, *needy* they are. They can't do much for themselves. They ask (ahem—*whine*) for help almost all the time. They don't pretend to be okay or care about what other people think. With most kids, what you see is what you get—emotions on their sleeves, along with a lot of well-expressed snot. Kids are great at depending on others. They're needy and they're fine with it. Do you believe that you're just as needy? We're not so comfortable admitting this. It's quite a shift for us to believe that God thinks neediness is beautiful.

But he does.

Jesus says our need is what qualifies us for his kingdom.

This means we don't have to resist the things that expose our need. Each one is an opportunity to know God more, not an obstacle keeping us from him. What does a child do when they fall and scrape their knees? They run into their mom's or dad's arms, tears streaming down their face, knowing they will find help. Kids embrace the one who will meet their needs. We can, too—*if* we dare to believe that God thinks our neediness, expressed through trust in him, is beautiful.

When we stumble and sin and fail *again*, instead of asking, "What is *wrong* with you?" God says, "I know exactly what's wrong with you. I know your greatest need. And I'm here to provide. That's what a good Father is for." How would things shift for us if we believed that God was *for* us, not against us? If we envisioned him as he truly is, our heavenly Father, ready to receive us into his arms—scrapes, tears, and all? I think we would actually come to him. Not buttoned up, but messy and real and needy.

We would learn what true humility is.

Jesus's Word to us is this: "Whoever humbles himself like this child is the greatest in the kingdom of heaven" (verse 4). Humility is admitting, *I am not God, and therefore, I need him.* We will grow in humility as we continue to see our great, ongoing dependence on him—one that arises as we fight our sin.

GOD TAKES YOUR SIN SERIOUSLY

How should God's people think about sin? Matthew 18 answers this question. Jesus spoke a lot about sin here, which tells us how important it is to confront. Our heavenly Father wants us to see the truth about ourselves, even when it's hard, and Jesus continues to press into it. Unless we call sin *sin,* we miss something vital about who God is and what he thinks of us as his people.

Take your sin seriously, Jesus says. "Truly, I say to you, unless you turn [from your sin] and become like children, you will never enter the kingdom of heaven" (verse 3). The word here for "turn" means "to repent" or "to change."[2] When the words "What's *wrong* with you?" fly from my mouth, Jesus commands me to turn from my sin. Not only this; he also gives me what I need to obey his command. He does the same for you. After you speak harsh words or lie to your spouse or look down on your friend or ogle something you shouldn't, and you wonder what God really thinks about you, remember "he sides with you against your sin."[3] He is not against you but for you, even though he opposes the sinful choices that threaten to destroy you. He wants to see you increasingly win battles along the way, even when this hurts:

> If your hand or your foot causes you to sin, cut it off and throw it away. It is better for you to enter life crippled or lame than with two hands or two feet to be thrown into the eternal fire. And if your eye causes you to sin, tear it out and throw it away. It is better for you to enter life with one eye than with two eyes to be thrown into the hell of fire. (verses 8–9)

Sin is serious, and God is seriously committed to rescuing us from it. Are we as committed to joining him in this lifelong effort?

Perhaps one of the reasons our assurance falters is that we've resigned ourselves to sin. *This is just the way I am*, we think. *I'll never change*. Or maybe change hasn't happened, because we don't think we need it. *I'm not that bad of a person*. But as we've already seen, we *can* change, and Jesus has purchased this gift through his precious blood.[4] When we are united to him by faith, we have everything we need to put away sin and pursue godliness—even when that imperfect pursuit involves some wandering along the way.

GOD PURSUES YOU

Because Jesus always seeks his straying sheep, we won't be lost for long.

If you're still not convinced about God's heart for you, hear the story Jesus told his disciples. He asked them, "What would you do in this situation?" A shepherd has one hundred sheep. One of them goes missing. So he leaves the ninety-nine to seek the one. Don't you wonder if you would do the same? A 1 percent loss doesn't seem too terrible. After all, time is money, and who has time to care about one foolish, straying sheep?

Who has time to deal with one more tantrum?

Who has energy for one more confrontation?

Who really cares about the poor, the oppressed, the widow, the childless?

Jesus does. He's not in a hurry, and he'll search all day long for the one.

So what does your heavenly Father think of you? He says you're worth pursuing. All his sheep are because "it is not [his] will . . . that one of these little ones should perish" (Matthew 18:14). Once Jesus, the Good Shepherd, has you in his tight grip, he refuses to let go. This doesn't mean you won't wander, because all of us do. But you can't wander too far from his seeking, redirecting, saving arms. Jesus said about his sheep, "No one will snatch them out of my hand" (John 10:28). With such a promise given, who could doubt his enduring, loving heart?

> Prone to wander, Lord, I feel it,
> Prone to leave the God I love.[5]

These words tell the tale of our journeys in these fallen frames. We're so quick to get distracted by the shininess of this world and all it offers that we lose sight of the true prize, our tender Shepherd. I see what others have—their bigger, nicer houses, their gifts and many opportunities, their seeming lack of discomfort and pain—and it's easy to wonder, *Do I actually have it better with Jesus?* But even when my heart strays from his path, he follows me with his goodness and mercy (Psalm 23:6). "Thus says the Lord GOD: Behold, I, I myself will search for my sheep and will seek them out" (Ezekiel 34:11). He reminds me that the answer to my question is undeniably, unequivocally *yes.*

Don't miss a second way the Good Shepherd pursues his sheep: He uses his church. He sends each one of us to seek the others and bring our fellow wanderers back. This is where Matthew 18 goes next. We gently and appropriately confront a brother's or sister's sin (verse 15), we approach the body of believers to help us reconcile and pursue holiness (verses 16–20), and we forgive seventy-seven times (verses 21–22) because we first have been forgiven (verses 23–35). That's why the church is never to be a place full of people with noses in the air, looking down on other sheep who wander. We are all wanderers at heart apart from the undeserved grace of Jesus. This realization moves us toward childlike humility as we draw near to others with the same grace and forgiveness we need every single day.

RETURN AND REJOICE

What happens when Jesus finds his sheep? What happens when you and I come back from the land of wandering and see, even if gradually, the truth about God in the face of our Shepherd? What happens when we realize, against everything we suspected, that there is no limit to God's relentless, pursuing love? We rejoice. *And so does Jesus.* "If he finds [his sheep], truly, I say to you, he rejoices over it more than over the ninety-nine that never went astray" (Matthew 18:13). Jesus rejoices over his rescued sheep, including you. *Yes, you.* This is not wishful thinking but an immovable reality that will swallow up your fear of rejection, if you will only run into your Father's arms and let him receive you.

And it's based not on what you've done but on what Jesus has done for you.

Now, *that* is something to take to heart. Something that will change you.

Meeting with Jesus

1. When it comes to how God sees you and what he thinks about you, which of these three truths (God thinks neediness is beautiful, sin is serious, and his sheep are worth pursuing) do you find hardest to believe? Why do you think this is? Read Luke 5:31–32, then journal about how these words of Jesus encourage you.
2. Think of a time when you fell into sin and felt either discouraged by it or tempted to brush it under the rug. What was your inner dialogue? What lies did you believe about God and yourself?
3. What might it look like for you to pursue another wandering sheep? Who in your family, church family, or neighborhood could use a gentle reminder of their spiritual need, the problem of sin, and the faithfulness of their Shepherd?

PART 3

LONELINESS

10

When You Need a Friend

Matthew 9:9–13

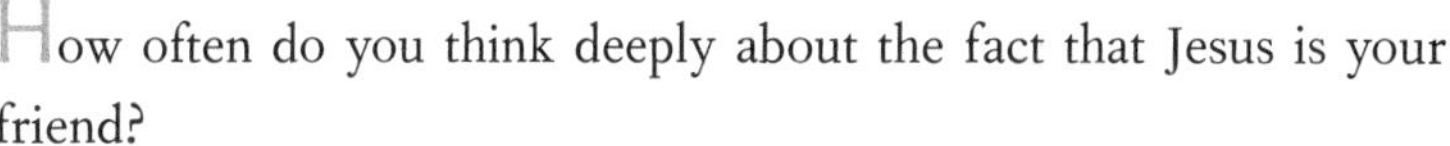

How often do you think deeply about the fact that Jesus is your friend?

Perhaps that's a new category—one that maybe feels inappropriate or overly casual. Beyond a doubt, Jesus is the undisputed King of kings and Lord of lords, our awesome Creator, and our Great High Priest. He is God, and there is no one like him. Holy beyond measure, Jesus is perfect in power, infinite in knowledge, and unmatched in wisdom.

And he is nearer than we know.

You may struggle to relate to Jesus as your friend, but the Bible has no problem with this category. Along with this, we see in Scripture how Jesus knows what it's like *not* to have friends. No one in the history of the world has been more misunderstood than Jesus. No one has been rejected as vehemently as he was, judged as wrongly, scorned as strongly, or abandoned as painfully. Alienation marked him. "He was despised and rejected," Isaiah writes. "We turned our backs on him and looked the other way" (Isaiah 53:3, NLT). The Gospels testify that, among other things, Jesus's days on earth were largely defined by loneliness (Matthew 8:20; John 1:11).[1] He gets us, for we, too, are lonely people.

We know the ever-deepening ache of singleness, that good desire for companionship that feels uncontrollably elusive. We know the sting of a marriage gone cold. We know the bitterness of being betrayed, the shame of being sidelined, the disappointment of being overlooked, the sadness of being alone in a crowd. In all of this, we may know that God is our Father, that he cares for us, but in a far-off sense. We're like a preteen girl who knows her parents sympathize with her but don't quite understand.

But Jesus? He knows what loneliness is, which makes him the most suitable friend.

OUR LONG-SUFFERING FRIEND

Have you ever really considered whom Jesus chose to hang around with? I'll bet we think of his disciples more highly than we should. The twelve men he chose were . . . not exactly friend material. They were a diverse group of unimpressive loudmouths and cheats, hotheads and doubters. He plucked Matthew from a tax collector's life of greed and theft, chose a lowly fisherman in Peter, and embraced a guy (Judas) who he knew would one day betray him. Enlisting misfits seems like the opposite of what God would do. But this is just what he did:

> As Jesus reclined at table in the house, behold, many tax collectors and sinners came and were reclining with Jesus and his disciples. And when the Pharisees saw this, they said to his disciples, "Why does your teacher eat with tax collectors and sinners?" (Matthew 9:10–11)

Shouldn't Jesus hang around with impressive types? No, in fact, the disciples were exactly the kind of people he came to surround himself with: messy sinners, just like us. To be a disciple of Jesus is to be a *learner.*[2] This is really spectacular news for us who are learning to trust God, as we stumble along the way and fall flat on our faces at times. It means Jesus is all in on this process. He's completely up for being a friend to unfinished, imperfect, and unreliable people like us. He's willing and, more than that, *invested* in the process.

He's a long-suffering friend.

His patient friendship means he is gentle and kind toward the unpolished you, the not-yet-there you. We've all known the limits of human patience—the annoyed sigh, the convenient excuse, the piercing comment, the straight-up rejection. But Jesus doesn't run out of patience. His bearing with us means the most because he *knows* the most.

He will be patient with you even as he tells you the painful truth about yourself.

OUR TRUTH-TELLING FRIEND

One of our pastors once asked his wife to give him one area where he could grow. Her response was to pause . . . and then ask, "Can I give you two?" Far better than the gentlest, most genuine spouse, Jesus is a truth-telling friend. He's the kind of friend who isn't scared of honesty, who refuses to flatter you, and who won't let you get away with foolishness, *because he cares so much*. The state of your soul matters to him. So he will tell you the truth:

> [The Pharisees] said to his disciples, "Why does your teacher eat with tax collectors and sinners?" But when [Jesus] heard it, he said, "Those who are well have no need of a physician, but those who are sick. Go and learn what this means: 'I desire mercy, and not sacrifice.' For I came not to call the righteous, but sinners." (Matthew 9:11–13)

All of us yearn for someone to tell us the truth—about ourselves and about reality. God created us with an ache to know what's right and real, and when his Son appeared, truth appeared in human form (John 1:14). Because we're longing for truth, we're actually longing for Jesus and the reality check he alone can give us. He's the friend who will tell us straight: We are sin-sick, and we need the healing he offers.

You can be offended by this, or you can be changed by it. A humble person receives his correction as a gift, not a curse. Peter couldn't stand Jesus's scary prediction about his upcoming death, but Jesus wouldn't have it: "Get behind me, Satan! . . . You are not setting your mind on the things of God, but on the things of man" (Matthew 16:23). Ouch. Peter might've scoffed at this, wounded by Jesus's hard words. But it seems he received it in truth.

What about us? Jesus doesn't leave his slow-learning disciples the same. He calls us in order to change us. And here's the beautiful thing: He doesn't do it all at once. He is merciful, patient, not in a hurry. Like a flashlight in a basement, he reveals specific areas of darkness within us bit by bit—not all at once, lest we grow discouraged and overwhelmed. He exposes our sin by degrees, and this is always his mercy. He cares about you too much to let you stay the same, for he is a truth-telling friend.

And after he exposes you, he will cover you because he is also a loyal friend.

OUR NEVER-FAILING FRIEND

I'll never forget my first experience with friend-abandonment. Right before the start of my sophomore year in high school, my closest girlfriend called to tell me we couldn't be friends anymore. She said she was moving on to better things. I was old news, and she wasn't afraid to dispose of me. She was kind enough to let me know in advance.

Thankfully, after I hung up the phone, I laughed. I had enough maturity to see how ridiculous this was, how petty, and yet I was still hurt. *What kind of a person does that?* An imperfect and unreliable one, with personal gain as their agenda. We may not be that forward with our selfishness, but how many times have we disappointed others? How often have we preferred to serve ourselves?

Even the most faithful friends are flawed. Even the most committed companions reach limits. Even the most reliable pals will fail us. But Jesus never will.

After Judas betrayed him to the religious leaders, none of Jesus's other disciples stuck up for him, and Peter denied even knowing him. This was more painful for Jesus than a "friend breakup" because, up to the last moment, his friends had insisted they would stay by his side (Matthew 26:35). But their good intentions failed when their loyalty was put to the test. So do ours. Still, Jesus is the kind of friend whose loyalty isn't deterred by sin.

Incredibly, the one thing that should ruin our friendship with Jesus is the exact thing he came to abolish. We are that terrible friend who says to him, "I want nothing to do with you," but Jesus insists on sticking by us. He went all the way to the cross to prove it, turning his enemies into friends. His work won't fail as he disarms the power of sin over us, freeing us for a life of imperfect discipleship and an eternity of perfect friendship.

So when the accuser digs up your old issues and shoves your sin in your face, show him your friend, Jesus. His blood has covered you, his holy record is yours, and he'll never leave your side. He's your never-failing friend.[3]

OUR LIFE-GIVING FRIEND

So often we look for life in our friendships. That's not all bad, since God created relationships so we won't be alone. A long walk or conversation with a close friend is incredibly life-giving to me, and my husband will tell you how I come home filled up and encouraged. But even my best friend isn't Jesus. No one can be who he is or provide everything he can. Here's the problem: If I look to imperfect people for life, I will be disappointed and crush them with my impossible expectations. But if I look to Jesus, I will find just the friend I'm looking for.

In the passage we've read, did you notice verse 13? Jesus said, "Go and learn what this means: 'I desire mercy, and not sacrifice.' For I came not to call the righteous, but sinners" (Matthew 9:13). What was he talking about? I love how *The Message* renders it: "Go figure out what this Scripture means: 'I'm after mercy, not religion.' I'm here to invite outsiders, not coddle insiders."

At one time or another, all of us feel like outsiders. So often we want people's approval. We want to be valued in their eyes, appreciated, celebrated, loved. And we'll do almost anything to earn this. But do you see the incredible truth God is telling us here? *Jesus makes outsiders insiders, giving us everything we most want.* He makes enemies into friends. He takes failures and forms disciples. And he does it all through his sheer, undeserved *mercy*. No hoops to jump through, no awards needed or merit earned, no proving yourself. Just mercy.

This means you can come to him as you are and receive from him everything you most need. What would it look like today for you to approach Jesus as your closest friend? Perhaps you focus so much on reverence for God that you've neglected proximity to him. Or maybe it's hard to relate to someone you can't physically see. How might it change the way you relate to Jesus if you imagined him sitting next to you or if you pictured him praying for you at God's right hand? How does it help to remember that Jesus has come to supply the very life and significance you're most desperate for?

Jesus is waiting to meet with you, as you are, right here and right now. He knows your loneliness. And through it all, he will be your unfailing friend.

Meeting with Jesus

1. In what ways have you experienced Jesus as a friend? Whether this is a new category for you or something familiar, what did you take away from this chapter? Read John 15:13–14 for further reflection.
2. To be a disciple of Jesus is to be a *learner.* How is Jesus inviting you to learn from him in this season?
3. Which aspect of Jesus's friendship (long-suffering, truth-telling, never-failing, life-giving) means the most to you today? Which do you hope to increasingly reflect in your own relationships with other people?

11

When You Feel Misunderstood

Mark 3:20–21, 31–35

I hung up the phone and felt the heat of anger rise within me as I replayed the conversation in my head. Not only had the person on the other end clearly misjudged what our family was enduring because of our son's neurodivergence, but she had also insinuated that I was exaggerating how difficult our situation was. As if the pain of our circumstances weren't enough, it was like being told to quit acting hurt as I stood there bleeding out, giving everything I had in order to survive.

I tried to convince myself that this person's hurtful words had come from a place of ignorance and misunderstanding, but the damage was done. Brick by brick, I began to build a wall of protection around my heart. If one person could so easily hurt me, regardless of the actual truth, then anyone could. In fact, I realized that those closest to me—relatives, church family, and friends—held the greatest power to hurt me.

Turns out, walls may block out potential hurt, but they also block out the community we were designed for.

The result? Loneliness.

I've felt it. Likely, you've felt it. None of us go through life unscathed by the pain of being hurt or misunderstood. It may have been an off-the-cuff comment that stung or a meticulously planned betrayal. Whatever it may be, it's left you wounded and angry.

Sadly, relational hurt is often most common—and most painful—within our physical or spiritual families. Sometimes it's over small misunderstandings when diverse personalities and perspectives clash. At times it comes from following Jesus when those we love think we're crazy. Other times it simply stems from the complexities of sinners in relationship with one another. Whatever the cause, the pain of being misunderstood or misjudged by those we love brings with it the gray skies of loneliness.

LIMITED UNDERSTANDING

I'm reminded of how Jesus's earthly family watched him go from *someone just like them* to a miracle-working prophet with a growing following. They saw him take his first shaky steps as a toddler. I imagine, given his virgin birth and sinless childhood, his parents and siblings *had* to know something was different about him. Somehow they still didn't understand.

Mark tells it like this: "Jesus entered a house, and again a crowd gathered, so that he and his disciples were not even able to eat. When his family heard about this, they went to take charge of him, for they said, 'He is out of his mind'" (Mark 3:20–21, NIV).

Not only did Jesus's family not understand who he really was, they thought he was crazy! The ones who had known him the longest understood him the least. They tried to make sense of his divine actions from an earthly perspective. So they jumped to the only conclusion that made sense to them: He must be off his rocker.

Of course, we aren't told how this made Jesus *feel*, but as discussed in the last chapter, his ministry was a lonely calling.

Because of that, he empathizes with you when a friend or family member hurls hurtful words your way or mocks your faith. He empathizes with you when you're slandered by someone you thought you could trust. He grieves with you when loved ones disappoint you or when others characterize you by past failure or sin rather than the growth God has worked within you.

Because he understands, you are *never* truly alone in these scenarios. You have a Savior who has known relational hurt to the uttermost. Instead of building a wall out of your pain, pour your hurt out to Jesus honestly, just as David does in Psalm 55:

> It is not an enemy who taunts me—
> then I could bear it;
> it is not an adversary who deals insolently with me—
> then I could hide from him.
> But it is you, a man, my equal,
> my companion, my familiar friend. . . .
>
> But I call to God,
> and the LORD will save me.
> Evening and morning and at noon
> I utter my complaint and moan,
> and he hears my voice. (verses 12–13, 16–17)

Jesus will never turn you away, even if others do.

WHO IS MY FAMILY?

All of us come from different backgrounds and family dynamics. Some have close-knit relationships with family, others are estranged, and some have never known their birth parents. Relation by blood doesn't always equate to the healthy experience God intended.

Thankfully, there's hope beyond the relationships that disappoint us. In fact, it's interesting how Jesus responded to the crowd in Mark 3 when he was told his family had arrived to speak with him:

> His mother and his brothers came, and standing outside they sent to him and called him. And a crowd was sitting around him, and they said to him, "Your mother and your brothers are outside, seeking you." And he answered them, "Who are my mother and my brothers?" And looking about at those who sat around him, he said, "Here are my mother and my brothers! For whoever does the will of God, he is my brother and sister and mother." (verses 31–35)

Was Jesus being dismissive and unloving to his family here? No, it's simply not in his nature.

Jesus is saying we're part of something greater and longer lasting than the family we're born into. His parents and siblings were bonded by blood, but his eternal family is bonded by the Spirit. Sadly, at least at one point in time, Jesus's brothers weren't in the family of God, which created a chasm between them. John 7:3–5 says, "His brothers said to him, 'Leave here and go to Judea so that your disciples can see your works that you are doing. For no one does anything in secret while he's seeking public recognition. If you do these things, show yourself to the world.' (For not even his brothers believed in him.)" (CSB).

Jesus's brothers misunderstood his mission. How it must have grieved the heart of Christ to see his own brothers' unbelief. Similarly, you may have family or friends you're close to in some ways, but your faith in Jesus means you speak a different language. No matter how much you try to find common ground, that core difference makes relational depth difficult.

That's what makes the family of God even sweeter. We're bonded by the Holy Spirit within us, not personality, shared culture, or earthly status. It lifts our eyes off our little world and reminds us that we're part of something bigger. I may struggle to connect to a sibling or other relative but then travel halfway across the world and experience an unspoken bond with another believer. At that moment, we may not know each other's customs, we may look different, and we may even be part of different church denominations. But that all fades to the background as we stand on the common ground of Jesus's undeserved grace and forgiveness.

Who are our true, eternally yoked brothers and sisters? "Whoever does the will of God, he is my brother and sister and mother" (Mark 3:35). In other words—the family of God.

Now, being in the family of God doesn't mean we'll always love one another well. Why? In part, because imposters posing as brothers and sisters cause division. But overall, because we're still in a family of sinful people. Forgiven sinners, yes. But sinners nonetheless. Even spiritual siblings quarrel.

I know many who have been deeply hurt by those in the church, and this grieves the heart of God. The family of God should be marked by grace, patience, justice, forgiveness, mercy, compassion, humility, and love. But too often we're far better at showing why we *need* Jesus than we are at *reflecting* him. Sadly, some of the deepest pain comes from within the body of Christ because we expect Christians to act like Christians. And too often we don't.

The truth is, as much as our brothers and sisters in Christ are a gift, they are never the basis of our hope. Jesus is. With him as our ultimate hope, we can rightly view the church (of which we're part) as a community of imperfect people in need of continual grace and forgiveness—not those who have already arrived.

GRACE RECEIVED, GRACE GIVEN

For most of my life, I've carried a sense of relational loneliness. Not long after I became a mom, one of our children began to struggle with neurodivergence that caused him to lash out uncontrollably—often without any clear reason. It became increasingly difficult to go out into public, and when I did, the disapproving and judgmental looks of others during his episodes only made me further retreat. To make matters worse, my home life became so beyond what most could comprehend and handle that I learned to protect others from my pain. It was too uncomfortable to endure their blank stare of shock after hearing about or seeing a fraction of my lived reality. Even those closest to me couldn't fully enter in, and it was easy to push people away because of it.

But in God's kindness, he has gradually humbled me through years of long-suffering. I've realized that before I can extend grace, I first need to acknowledge my own need for it. The truth is, we're all ignorant in some ways. It's easy to make sweeping assumptions about others until you find yourself faced with the complexities of a life-changing situation that sucks the pride right out of you.

I remember seeing a child throwing a tantrum in a parking lot and assuming, *Wow, there's clearly no discipline there.* Now, after years of navigating life with a neurodivergent child, I'm quicker to feel compassion than jump to criticism. It's far better for me to silently pray for that parent than to throw stones with my limited understanding. I can extend grace because I know how desperately I need grace.

I believe most insensitive comments and assumptions aren't maliciously intended but stem from ignorance, immaturity, and pride. But even when they are intentional, we can pray honestly to the Lord:

> *Jesus, you know the hurt I feel. You know how those words stung and how easily I could let anger and bitterness take root right now. Thank you that you see and know everything, even when I lack the right words to ex-*

plain it. I know I have not always understood and been gracious toward others, and I need you to help me extend grace and forgiveness to this person, just as you have shown me in the past. Thank you that I'm not really alone, even when this world and my circumstances make me feel otherwise. Please be near to me. Amen.

God will never turn away a heart that turns to him in need.

Here's what's amazing: The same brothers who doubted Jesus ended up writing New Testament letters (James 1:1; Jude 1), and one became a leader in the church (Acts 1:14; 15:13–21; 1 Corinthians 15:7). Jesus showed his family mercy, and ultimately many of them believed. With Christ, even though it's not a guarantee, we can hope for healed relationships.

Are you feeling the loneliness of relational hurt? Do you feel misunderstood by those around you? You aren't alone. Jesus has been there, and he'll meet you there now. Family and friends will let us down. Pastors will let us down. The church will let us down. And yes, *we* will let others down as well.

But take heart: Jesus never will.

Meeting with Jesus

1. Is there someone who has hurt or misjudged you? How have you responded?
2. Read Hebrews 13:6 and Proverbs 29:25, then reflect on how Jesus never misunderstands you or fails you. How does this free you from the need for approval from others?
3. Are you struggling with continued bitterness because of past hurt? Share with the Lord where you are struggling with the pain caused by another, and ask for his help to love them and forgive with his strength.

12

When You Worry That You're Not a Real Christian

Mark 15:33–34

What is your greatest fear? There are a number of things high on my list that bother me and disturb my thoughts. I worry about our family, the fragility of my health, my kids' choices, unexpected tragedies—things I can't control. But there's one that trumps the rest.

I'm terrified of not knowing Jesus.

I'm not talking about information: I know a lot about Jesus. I'm talking about relationship, presence, *closeness*. I'm afraid of standing before him someday and hearing those bone-chilling words: "I never knew you; depart from me" (Matthew 7:23). I'm afraid that after decades of following him, serving him, parenting and writing and teaching for him, the final verdict from his lips will be "Who are you?"

Does this resonate with you? Maybe, like me, you wonder about your spiritual state. You worry you're not *really* close to him. Or maybe this book has challenged you to know Jesus as a real person, and this is new for you—so now you're wondering where you stand. My focus in this chapter is the loneliness we feel *from Jesus*, the spiritual distance that often plagues us and makes us question, *Do I really know him? Does he know me?*

Is our relationship with Jesus for real? Or is it all a sham?

GOD'S HEART AT CALVARY

To address our concerns, we'll attempt to plumb some of the depths of one of the Bible's greatest mysteries: the death of God's Son on the cross. Wherever you're coming from, I want you to see that *what happened then* relates to your walk with Jesus right now. I want you to see that you can't grow closer to him as God until you grasp what he did for you *in the flesh, as a person*, here on earth.

But wait, you may be thinking. *I already know about the cross. Jesus died for my sins there.* The cross feels familiar, perhaps even boring. Or you might be hesitant because you haven't thought much about Jesus's death at all. But this meditation is entirely worth our time, for when we stare at the cross, we see more of the loveliness of God's heart for us. To do this, we'll answer two questions: *What happened at the cross? And how do I know God actually loves me?*

WHAT HAPPENED AT THE CROSS?

My kids and I were reading a Scripture passage the other day. (And by "my kids and I," I mean that I was reading while they were squirming in their seats and talking over me. We're working on it.) I sometimes ask them questions to make sure they're listening, so I said, "What happened at the cross?" My older daughter, with hardly a pause, answered, "Jesus died for our sins." Now, I've got to say, this proud mom was pleased by her answer. *Ding ding ding!* For a young child, this is an excellent response, a solid grasp of what theologians call the Atonement.

But is there more? How would *you* answer this question?

Yes, Jesus died for our sins. But what exactly does this mean? Let's read Mark's account of the Crucifixion to see what happened as Jesus died:

> When the sixth hour had come, there was darkness over the whole land until the ninth hour. And at the ninth hour Jesus cried with a loud voice, "Eloi, Eloi, lema sabachthani?" which means, "My God, my God, why have you forsaken me?" (Mark 15:33–34)

Darkness. In the middle of the day. A total blackout at noon. Was this a storm, a coincidence of severe weather? No. God turned out the lights.[1] This wasn't mere theatrics; this was heaven's courtroom breaking into Calvary. God's judgment, however, wasn't aimed at the murderers—it was falling on his Son. In Jesus's dying agony, he cried the words of Psalm 22: "Why have you forsaken me?" (verse 1).

The great mystery is how these words could possibly come from Jesus's mouth, from the One who only ever spoke God's truth, trusted God's ways, and knew God's love. Why would God refuse to rescue his perfect Son? Because, in that moment, Jesus embodied all the evil of humanity, "the living excrement from our souls."[2] Jesus bore in his body all our sins, and this changed him into a black hole of wickedness (1 Peter 2:24). His suffering on the cross involved far more than physical anguish. There he absorbed God's anger toward our sin and his abandonment because of it.

We wonder about God's love in all of this. How could a loving Father possibly do such a thing to his Son, pouring out his wrath and forsaking him? But remember, this was always the plan from the very beginning. As we learned in chapter 2, Jesus became like us so we will become like him, and yes—he even became sin for us

(2 Corinthians 5:21).[3] He was *that* committed to our rescue. Like a dynamic trio linking arms in spiritual battle, our heavenly Father and his dear Son, through the infinite love of the Spirit, agreed to save the world. No one was forced; everyone was willing, and it was all for love.

> In that old rugged cross, stained with blood so divine,
> A wondrous beauty I see,
> For 'twas on that old cross Jesus suffered and died,
> To pardon and sanctify me.[4]

Jesus went where we were headed, into the dust of death, so that we could go where he alone deserves to be, raised to life in heaven. Hell is the total and unending absence of God's love and all the good his love produces. If hell is God-forsakenness, then Jesus endured hell for us on the cross. This is what happened there as his Father looked away from him. This is what Jesus did there—and he did it for you.

He treasures you so much, he went to hell in your place.

HOW DO I KNOW GOD ACTUALLY LOVES ME?

So often our experience here on earth feels like a degree of hell. We feel so alone. *If God loves me so much*, we wonder, *then why has he left me to fend for myself?* He seems so far away at times, and we question if we really know him and if he knows us. And if he knows us, we conclude, then he must not like what he knows. What do we do with all the distance we feel from Jesus?

We look at it through Calvary's lens. We let God's love displayed at the cross interpret our experience, rather than letting our experience interpret his love.

Let's do this right now in two realms of spiritual loneliness.

Spiritual Uncertainty

First, there's the loneliness that comes from a lack of assurance of salvation. We're discouraged by our ongoing struggle against sin, we're allured by the world (even if we don't want to be), and our enemy Satan has a destructive agenda. The Christian life can feel so hard that we wonder if we're going to make it. Is our faith in Jesus strong enough to last to the end? Are we the real deal? Or does all of this mean we aren't?

Be encouraged—the presence of a spiritual struggle indicates spiritual *life*.

Even as we struggle to hold on to Jesus, there he is, holding on to us. Even as we wander away from him, there he is, guiding us back. Even as we're uncertain about where we stand before him, there he is, reassuring our worried hearts:

> My sheep hear my voice, and I know them, and they follow me. I give them eternal life, and they will never perish, and *no one will snatch them out of my hand.* My Father, who has given them to me, is greater than all, and no one is able to snatch them out of the Father's hand. I and the Father are one. (John 10:27–30)

So when you worry your faith isn't strong enough to save you, rest assured—it's not. *But Jesus is.* You've been rescued not by the strength of your resolve but by the strength of your Savior, who resolved to rescue you. He did so at the cost of his own life, by willingly giving himself over to desertion by his Father and to death itself. The One who perished on the cross couldn't be held by the grave, and now his nail-scarred hands hold on to you.

Let Jesus's strong grip be your comfort and reassurance. No one and nothing will snatch you from his hands.

Spiritual Dryness

Then there's spiritual dryness, a common experience for believers through the ages. In these seasons, God feels far away from us. For me this has been cyclical, and it's usually related to my circumstances. The Lord has made us intricate, holistic beings, and there's a definite connection between bodily, mental, and spiritual health. For example, in particularly tough seasons of chronic pain, it's harder for me to persevere in seeking Jesus; I'm so worn out and weary that a kind of spiritual depression sets in. "When you are exhausted," Don Whitney says, "you may not feel very spiritual, and that can distort your perception of the Lord's presence and blessing."[5] Other times (or maybe at the same time), our fickle hearts are simply drawn away from Jesus because we desire worldly things. In all these times, a spiritual pruning is taking place.

As Jesus encouraged his disciples, hard seasons of spiritual pruning are meant to make us more fruitful: "I am the true vine, and my Father is the vinedresser. Every branch in me that does not bear fruit he takes away, and every branch that does bear fruit he prunes, that it may bear more fruit" (John 15:1–2). When we are connected to Jesus, the vine, even in painful or low-fruit-bearing seasons we can rest assured he is working, producing something good in us. Similarly, although the cross of Christ wasn't good in itself, it shouts that God is near and active as he works out his goodness through hardship, including our seasons of spiritual dryness.

The question for us is, Are we still choosing to abide in Jesus when the going gets hard? When seasons of dryness hit and we can't *feel* the presence of God, will we still remain with him? This might mean continuing to sit in Scripture, even when the words feel stale. It might mean continuing to talk to God in prayer, even when our words feel weak. These two things, Scripture and prayer, strengthen us to abide—because he alone is our life and there is nowhere else we can go.

There are also spiritually lonely times when God removes a *conscious sense* of his nearness, what Christians in history have called "God's desertions."[6] Whitney notes that in these times we *perceive* that God is far away, even though he is actually very near.[7] But Jesus's promise to his disciples holds true for those who love him: "Behold, I am with you always, to the end of the age" (Matthew 28:20). Perhaps God is strengthening us so we will learn to walk by faith and not by feelings, and maybe he is revealing to us in a fresh way how it is good to be near to him (Psalm 73:28).

God Actually Loves Us

When God's presence feels far away, when we wonder if our relationship with Jesus is the real deal, when we're spiritually lethargic, when we're struggling to put one foot before the other in our walk with him, when we fear our faith may fail, God's love is fully displayed at the cross. There Jesus was forsaken so we will never be, and *this* is how we know God actually loves us.

When God's Son cried out to him for relief, there was no response—only a hidden face.

Because of him, our faces will never be ashamed (Psalm 34:5).

Instead, we will be radiant reflections of his lavish love.

Meeting with Jesus

1. When have you felt far away from Jesus? How would you describe this spiritual loneliness? Which of the above factors might have been at play during that season (spiritual uncertainty, spiritual dryness)?
2. In your own words, how would you answer the following questions:
   - What happened at the cross?
   - How do you know God actually loves you?
3. Which of Jesus's promises (Matthew 28:20; John 10:27–30; 15:1–2) do you need to hold on to today? In what ways do they reassure you of his unfailing love?

PART 4

PAIN

13

When You Want to Be Healed

Matthew 9:5–8

I rolled my aching body onto its side and squinted as the sunrays beamed through the slivers of space between the blinds. The sun, which used to represent the hope of a new dawn, now taunted me—a reminder of the life I wasn't living. It had been seven weeks of an agonizing illness and five weeks of being completely bedridden.

As the hours ticked by at a miserably slow pace and the days turned to weeks, my desperate pleas for healing seemed trapped in an echo chamber. Why was God silent? Didn't he know there were four kids who needed their mom back, and a husband struggling to manage life as a single parent?

"God, why do you keep me alive if you won't allow me to truly live?" I lamented.

As the weeks continued, I found myself in an endless sea of questions, doubts, and well-intentioned but unhelpful comments from others. "Have you prayed for your healing and truly believed Jesus will bring it? You know, Jesus has already declared and promised your healing—you just have to claim it as yours."

Is my faith too weak? I wondered. *Has Jesus* really *promised my healing on earth?*

This wasn't the first time I'd wrestled with these questions—or the first time I'd felt shamed into believing my continued suffering was due to a lack of faith. Chronic illness and pain, in one form or another, have been part of me for as long as I can remember. They've affected the choices I've made and paths I've taken. They've robbed me of countless things I would have enjoyed—activities, time with others, simple pleasures, and memories that others made without me. But more than anything else, they've caused me to wonder why Jesus so often healed those who searched for his healing hand but has yet to heal me.

Can you relate?

If you've battled any kind of lengthy illness or pain, you've most likely had people assure you that your healing is guaranteed on this earth if you pray without doubting. But as time passes and the pain remains, these whispers just add to your confusion.

THE PURPOSE OF JESUS'S EARTHLY HEALINGS

Did Jesus *really* promise earthly healing to all who call on him in faith? If not, what hope do we have in the middle of pain?

There's no sugarcoating the vast implications of debilitating illness and pain. Physical suffering is one of the most difficult to endure. You can't distract yourself from it. You can't take a vacation from it. And it leaves no area of life untouched. Bodily pain will bring even the strongest to their knees.

Pain drives me in desperation to Jesus like nothing else does. No one can see or stop the pain radiating within me. In such a helpless state, I can only cry out to the One who can see what others can't and who has the power to do something about it.

And yet my prayers are often not met with physical relief, even though I know Jesus can heal me in an instant. Over the years, that tension has sent me searching Scripture for answers, and I've found encouragement in passages like Matthew 9: "Some men brought to [Jesus] a paralyzed man, lying on a mat. When Jesus saw their faith, he said to the man, 'Take heart, son; your sins are forgiven' " (verse 2, NIV).

Immediately, his response upset the religious leaders. Physical healing was one thing. But having the boldness to claim forgiveness of sins? That was too far.

Knowing their thoughts, Jesus responded,

> "Which is easier: to say, 'Your sins are forgiven,' or to say, 'Get up and walk'? But so that you may know that the Son of Man has authority on earth to forgive sins"—then he told the paralytic, "Get up, take your stretcher, and go home." So he got up and went home. When the crowds saw this, they were awestruck and gave glory to God, who had given such authority to men. (verses 5–8, CSB)

Jesus was peeling back the curtain because he knows we're shortsighted. He knows we'd be content to have our physical ailments relieved, even if it means remaining blissfully unaware of the eternal suffering we're headed toward.

So Jesus challenged our shortsighted view of his miracles by asking, "Which is easier: to say, 'Your sins are forgiven,' or to say, 'Get up and walk'?" The latter would bring physical healing that wouldn't last. The former would be invisible but would last forever. Jesus tells us plainly why he chose to miraculously heal on earth: "So that you may believe that Jesus is the Christ, the Son of God, and that by believing you may have life in his name" (John 20:31).

Physical healing was a signpost—a pointer to Jesus's *greater* ability to heal souls.

It was a means to a greater end, not an end in itself.

To me, that's a comfort when the nagging doubts tell me, "If you only had enough faith, maybe he'd grant your request for healing like he did for the paralytic." Instead, Jesus's words tell a different story. Physical healing isn't the measuring stick of God's love or a sign of the strength of my faith.

After all, no one prayed with a more desperate cry of faith than Jesus did in Gethsemane. Do we dare accuse Jesus of failing to pray in faith? Absolutely not! In his spirit, he was willing. Though in his humanity, he cried out to his Father in agony, pleading to be spared from the horrors of the cross, God said no. "The way of suffering was the Father's plan."[1]

Here's what we need to see: God didn't deny Jesus's request because he lacked faith. To the contrary. Jesus showed the greatest display of faith ever known to mankind—trusting his Father's perfect will *more* than he desired relief.

THE PROBLEM WITH PAIN

Thankfully, Jesus understands how desperately we want to escape the physical pain of this world. He wasn't spared from the skinned knees of childhood, the cold sweat of a fever, or the pain of nails being driven through his hands, and he personally knew the ache of betrayal, physical abuse, and the loss of loved ones. He doesn't sit idly by, caring about our eternal souls but not our physical beings. He hurts with us in our pain, knowing the ailments that plague us are a constant reminder that this world isn't as it was meant to be. Although God can redeem it, pain itself isn't good.

Just as salvation from our sins doesn't free us from the struggle of sin, Jesus's redeeming power doesn't mean we'll no longer suffer in this life. As followers of Jesus, our pain isn't evidence of God's displeasure or a lack of faith; it's a physical reminder that we live in a sin-stricken world.

HAS GOD PROMISED EARTHLY HEALING?

I've heard it more times than I can count. No doubt you have as well. Maybe you've even said it to others:

> If you're a Christian, you simply need to have faith and claim Jesus's healing power. After all, God said in Isaiah 53:5, "He was pierced for our transgressions; he was crushed for our iniquities; upon him was the chastisement that brought us peace, and with his wounds we are healed."

Sounds good at face value, but in reality, it's a misinterpretation of Scripture that offers a false promise.

By believing this falsehood, we place a burdensome expectation on others or ourselves that Jesus himself never did. Does faith matter? Yes! As Margaret Clarkson says, "When asking for healing, we must ask in faith . . . but we must always remember that our faith in itself is no more the means of our healing than it is of our salvation. Faith is necessary for both, but it is God who does the work."[2]

Friend, it's easy to misinterpret verses like Isaiah 53:5 to match our desires. But if we look at them in the context of Scripture, we see how a spiritual, eternal promise can mistakenly be twisted into a physical, shortsighted one. In other words, we wield the name of Jesus to bend God's will to our agenda.

But consider the practical implications of this misinterpretation: If Jesus promised physical healing to all who claim it by faith, no believer would ever die. We would keep claiming our healing in the name of Jesus. Every ailment that comes our way would have to be healed if that's what his sacrifice was meant to accomplish. And yet some faithful believers battle chronic illness their entire lives; some fall terminally ill and, despite the faith-filled prayers of many, pass through death into glory.

Did God fail to heal them? No.

He simply chose to heal them fully and eternally, rather than physically and temporarily.

Can God heal us if he chooses to? Yes, by his grace—even miraculously at times. But whether he chooses to bring earthly healing or not, his purpose will *always* be a deeper work of healing—bringing our dead hearts to life and growing us to know, love, and reflect more of him. One brings momentary relief until the next ailment plagues us. The other brings lasting change that can't be taken from us.

EXPECT HIS FAITHFULNESS

Let me be clear: It's *not* wrong to desire healing, and it's *not* wrong to pray—even plead—for earthly healing and relief, knowing Jesus still grants miracles. But if our hope rises and falls with the ups and downs of continued pain, we won't just question Jesus's ways—we'll question his heart. So Jesus charges us in Luke 18:1 to not lose heart as we pray with persistence. We have freedom to use whatever means God provides to improve our situation but always with a heart that accepts what he allows as what's best for us.

At times, it's God's severe mercy to not immediately grant every prayer for relief and healing. Not because he's indifferent to our pain, but because he intends to redeem it in ways we can't yet see. He's chiseling away at our earthly way of thinking, giving us eyes to see the faithfulness of his sustaining grace, rather than solely the answers we seek. Little by little, as we trust our frail earthly frames to Jesus in faith, he will draw us closer to the heart of God, sustaining us with his strength. He may give us more than *we think we can handle*, but he will never give us more than *he will equip us to handle* in his strength.

JESUS'S HEART IS FOR US

Pain may tempt us to believe otherwise, but Jesus's heart is entirely for us. Even as we acknowledge that God's ways are often not our ways, the heart of our Father is never to grieve his children (Lamentations 3:33). The same Jesus who was stirred to compassion by the lame and sick is moved by your pain and cries for relief.

As Joni Eareckson Tada wrote, "God permits what he hates to achieve what he loves."[3]

God hates when his children suffer. I believe it grieved him to watch me lie in agony for weeks. And it grieves him to see the pain that you or your loved one longs to be free from right now. But at times, just like with Jesus's death on the cross, he allows pain for a greater purpose. Just as there was greater work to be done through the cross, sometimes there's greater work to be done through our suffering than in the removal of it.

I encourage you to pray earnestly and honestly to your heavenly Father for your earthly healing. If this is his will, it will happen because he knows this is best for you. You can work to improve your situation with all the resources God has graciously provided in this world. But as you wait, if you don't experience healing in your timing or way, know that God is allowing something he hates (your pain) for the sake of achieving something he loves—a deeper healing that this world can never give to you and never take from you.

Meeting with Jesus

1. If Jesus were standing before you today, what ailment would you bring to him, asking for his healing touch? Bring your desire for healing to him today, trusting that he's willing and able, if it's what's best for you right now.
2. What have you believed or been taught about what Jesus's healings in the New Testament mean for us today? What are your greatest doubts, questions, or challenges that have stemmed from that belief? Journal your answers.
3. When has God not brought the healing you desire but instead done a deeper work in you as a result? Read Romans 5:3–5 and spend a few moments thanking him for how he's changed and sustained you.

14

When You're Weary of Waiting on God

John 11:1–44

It had been eight months of painful waiting. The impacts of a pandemic had swept across the world, taking my husband's job along with so much else. With bills piling up, growing needs, and no income, panic began to set in. Every promising job opportunity came to a screeching halt for reasons so outrageous that you'd think it was a cruel comedy. God seemed silent, the future looked bleak, and we were desperate.

Then the phone rang. What began as an unexpected conversation between my husband and an old college buddy led to a cross-country road trip from Chicago to Colorado to explore a job opportunity. By the end of that week, my husband had a job and we had a new home. Thirty days later, we were living in a new state and a new house, trying to adjust to circumstantial whiplash.

That season wasn't the first or last lengthy season of God's delays. And despite the ways I've seen his past faithfulness, I'm still not a fan of waiting. I've yet to meet someone who enjoys waiting, especially when that waiting involves enduring something painful.

Maybe the needs are great, but the more you plead for relief, the challenges only multiply. You've spent years praying for a prodigal child, but the longer you wait, the more hopeless things appear. Or maybe you or a loved one is battling an illness, and despite the prayers of many, the hope of healing looks bleaker by the day.

In these disorienting seasons, I've often found myself asking, "God, where are you? Don't you care that I'm suffering so deeply? If you love me and can do something about it, why do you seem indifferent to my cries for relief?" Oh, how agonizing these seasons are. God's apparent silence is a difficult reality. It's unsettling and faith-shaking, and if we're honest, it's easier to distract ourselves and push aside the questions and confusion rather than face them.

But face them we must.

THE MYSTERY OF HIS DELAYS

So much of the Christian life runs counter to our natural way of thinking. God knows how difficult it is to have faith without sight. As limited, shortsighted beings, learning to trust a limitless, eternally minded God is simply *not natural* for us.

But in God's kindness, he's given us insight into his character and heart through the life of Jesus. The Gospels give us a relatable bird's-eye view of interactions that perplexed even the most faithful followers of Jesus. John 11 is one account that has been profoundly helpful to me in my own perplexing seasons of waiting. John tells it like this:

> A certain man was ill, Lazarus of Bethany, the village of Mary and her sister Martha. It was Mary who anointed the Lord with ointment and wiped his feet with her hair, whose brother Lazarus was ill. So the sisters sent to him, saying, "Lord, he whom you love is ill." But when Jesus heard it he said, "This illness does not lead to death. It is for the glory of God, so that the Son of God may be glorified through it."

> Now Jesus loved Martha and her sister and Lazarus. So, when he heard that Lazarus was ill, he stayed two days longer in the place where he was. (verses 1–6)

I'm sorry—what? Those last two sentences seem to contradict each other. If Jesus *really* loved Martha, Mary, and Lazarus, why would he delay? He knew how desperately they needed him. He knew he had power to heal his friend and save many from the grief they were heading toward. But he delayed anyway. Even more confusing? Jesus said that the illness wouldn't lead to death, which *would* have been reassuring except for one problem: Lazarus died.

Finally, after four long days, Jesus showed up.

Interestingly, we see Mary and Martha handle Jesus's return in completely different ways here: "When Martha heard that Jesus was coming, she went and met him, but Mary remained seated in the house. Martha said to Jesus, 'Lord, if you had been here, my brother would not have died. But even now I know that whatever you ask from God, God will give you' " (verses 20–22).

Martha responded by running to Jesus with an honest mix of confusion and faith.

She was right. If Jesus had been there, her brother wouldn't have died. Understandably, she was perplexed. And yet, amazingly, she still believed Jesus had the power to save him.

Mary, on the other hand, didn't move an inch.

Scripture doesn't specify what was going through Mary's mind, but it isn't hard to theorize. If I were her, I would have been wondering, *Doesn't Jesus love my brother, Lazarus? Doesn't he love me? I sacrificially anointed Jesus with expensive ointment and wiped his feet with my hair. Couldn't he have at least done this one thing for me?* Jesus could have saved her brother, but he chose not to. He delayed—and if we didn't know the end of the story, we'd have every reason to lose heart.

We've all experienced something that's caused us to wonder, *If Jesus* can, *why* hasn't *he?*

Thankfully, this wasn't the end of their story. And it's not the end of ours either.

IS JESUS INDIFFERENT?

It's comforting to remember the humanity of Jesus here. Yes, he was fully God. Yes, he had a good plan in store for those he loved. But it didn't negate the fact that he knew his delay would wound his friends. I believe that's why this passage mentions Jesus's love for Martha, Mary, and Lazarus several times. There aren't many places where the Gospels point out Jesus's love for specific individuals. However, John goes out of his way to make the point. From our vantage point, Jesus's actions seem opposite of loving. But God seems to be both acknowledging and challenging our human understanding of love here. He's acknowledging it in the sense that Jesus, in his humanity, had close friendships just as we do. Because of that, he must have agonized over the distress his delay caused his dearly loved friends.

On the flip side, he's challenging our shortsighted human understanding of love. I imagine Jesus was feeling a lot like the parent who bears the pain of their child's cries, despite knowing there's something better in store if they'd only wait and trust their love for them.

But our understanding of love is conditioned by our longing for immediate gratification and relief. God's love, on the other hand, is far beyond what we can comprehend. In his kindness, he's given us teachings like this and circumstances that challenge our small view of love in order to grow our capacity for a love that is deeper, wider, and unlike the fickle affections of this world.

And *that* is precisely what Jesus did next in John 11:

> Jesus said to [Martha], "Your brother will rise again." Martha said to him, "I know that he will rise again in the resurrection on the last day." Jesus said to her, "I am the resurrection and the life. Whoever believes in me, though he die, yet shall he live, and everyone who lives and believes in me shall never die. Do you believe this?" She said to him, "Yes, Lord; I believe that you are the Christ, the Son of God, who is coming into the world." (verses 23–27)

Jesus, although pained by the grief of his delay, had something far greater to give those he loved—showing his power and authority over death itself. His temporary delay may have brought short-term confusion and hurt, but in the end, it was part of a greater plan.

That was beyond momentary love. It was the actions of a man who loved so deeply, he was willing to allow short-term pain for life-changing and eternal gain.

TRUST THE SAVIOR WHO WEEPS

Finally, we come to one of the most beautiful moments of the story:

> When Mary came to where Jesus was and saw him, she fell at his feet, saying to him, "Lord, if you had been here, my brother would not have died." When Jesus saw her weeping, and the Jews who had come with her also weeping, he was deeply moved in his spirit and greatly troubled. And he said, "Where have you laid him?" They said to him, "Lord, come and see." Jesus wept. (verses 32–35)

Those final two words carry so much weight.

We'll delve more deeply into this in a later chapter, but in our pain and grief, Jesus weeps with us, even when he knows the good plan he has in store for us. It's remarkable, really. He knew the end of the story, yet he was still deeply moved and greatly troubled. Mary's and Martha's pain was his pain. And so is ours.

Jesus knows the glorious end of your story, yet he still weeps with you in the sorrow and pain of the in-between.

WAIT WITH ANTICIPATION

Friend, what are you waiting for right now? What pain are you experiencing as a result of God's delays? Be encouraged by the truth that God never disappoints those who wait on him (Lamentations 3:25), just as Mary and Martha experienced firsthand:

> Jesus said to [Martha], "Did I not tell you that if you believed you would see the glory of God?" So they took away the stone. And Jesus lifted up his eyes and said, "Father, I thank you that you have heard me. I knew that you always hear me, but I said this on account of the people standing around, that they may believe that you sent me." When he had said these things, he cried out with a loud voice, "Lazarus, come out." The man who had died came out, his hands and feet bound with linen strips, and his face wrapped with a cloth. Jesus said to them, "Unbind him, and let him go." (John 11:40–44)

If you believe, you will see the glory of God. It's a theme that can be traced throughout all of Scripture. There are countless biblical accounts where the middle of the story seemed confusing, chaotic, hurtful, or impossible, until the glory of God shone through the very things that seemed hopeless.

Abraham and Sarah were infertile before God brought the promised offspring (Genesis 21).

Joseph was rejected by his family, sold into slavery, and thrown into prison before he was raised to power at the exact time God chose to use him to save countless lives (Genesis 37; 39–45).

Ruth lost her husband and security before she was led to Boaz, the man whom God used to redeem what she had lost, ultimately giving Ruth the privilege of carrying on the lineage that led to Jesus (Ruth 1–4).

David was anointed future king, only to find himself running for his life and hiding in caves. It was a long and painful training ground before he sat on a throne, made ready by God to be a humble king fit to lead his people (1 Samuel 16–31).

And Paul was tortured, shipwrecked, imprisoned, and rejected for sharing the gospel, yet generations of believers have been changed by his testimony and example of faith (2 Corinthians 11:23–27).

Right now you may feel like Abraham and Sarah in their infertility, Joseph in prison, Ruth grieving her husband and sense of belonging, David hiding in a cave, Paul being mistreated, or Mary weeping at Lazarus's tomb. But you and I serve the same God who was at work in each of their stories to do far more than they could see or imagine.

Whether you're grieving a loss, crying out in pain, or struggling to understand why God may be withholding something that seems good or needed, this isn't the end of the story. Jesus is committed to what's best for you, but he equally cares for your heart in the process. We see Jesus's heart for his hurting children all throughout his time on earth. It's as if he's saying to us through each interaction, "*Trust me, my child. You can't yet see the whole story as I do, but I have promised good, and I am actively bringing it about. Yet even though I know the end of the story, I feel and carry your pain, confusion, and grief as if they're my own. I don't desire your pain, but I love you enough to allow this temporary heartache for your greater and lasting good and to display my glory through it. Trust my heart for you more than what you can see, and know without a doubt that you will see the glory of God.*"

One day it will all be made clear. Until then, trust the heart of the Father, who knows the end of the story.

Meeting with Jesus

1. What are you waiting on the Lord for right now? What questions, fears, or doubts have come up while you wait?
2. Which sister's response do you relate to more in this story? (Martha immediately ran to Jesus in her confusion. Mary sat alone, struggling to reconcile his delay in her heart.)
3. Jesus has shown that there are purposes within the mystery of his delays, but he's also shown that he weeps with us in the pain of his delays. Which of these truths most encourages you today as you wait on him? Write out Psalm 130:5–6 and tape it somewhere that you will see it on a daily basis.

15

When You're Desperate for Change

Mark 5:24–34

"All of your results came back normal."

This was good news, but nonetheless it left me deflated. Every specialist had said the same thing, followed by raised eyebrows and another set of discouraging words: "Maybe you're just stressed?" Perplexed by yet another report of seemingly good health, I left the endocrinologist's office at a dead end. Where do you turn when everyone's insisting you're okay but you're absolutely not and you know it?

Anyone facing chronic pain knows the discouragement of prolonged medical inquiries with few answers. You might know the strange desire to be told that, yes, something is indeed wrong with you—because at least this news brings closure and a confirmation you're not crazy. You might know the hard and exhausting road of answer-seeking, only to find none. Or maybe you found an answer—finally, a reason for your pain!—but after many treatments, you haven't found the healing you're looking for.

Maybe the person hurting is not you but someone you love. It's a helpless feeling to stand on the sidelines and watch a family member or friend suffer. You wish you could take their pain and make it all better. But you can't.

Inexplicable and frustrating, chronic illness leaves us desperate. We feel like the bleeding woman who dared to touch Jesus.

DARING TO TOUCH JESUS

She trailed behind the crowd, uncertain if she should approach. The mass of people surrounding him overwhelmed her. She couldn't see what he was doing or where he was going, and she couldn't hear him speak. She'd heard the amazing reports about Jesus: healing, demon-expulsion, and other miracles. She needed a miracle. It had been twelve long years of incessant blood flow, like her life was draining away slowly. And along with it, her savings, her possessions, her strength, and any hope that things would ever change.

Here, standing before her, was the man they said was a miracle worker, a change maker, the one who could cause impossible things to happen. This was Jesus of Nazareth. She caught a glimpse of his face, and something compelled her to move toward the crowd. Inching closer, she lingered on the edge of the busy circle.

A man said Jesus was on his way to heal someone's daughter. *So I have this one chance*, she thought, *this one opportunity before Jesus disappears inside the girl's house*. Under her breath, she uttered her conviction: "If I touch even his garments, I will be made well" (Mark 5:28).

For twelve long years, she had been waiting for Jesus, but she hadn't known it until this moment. Now here he was, standing right in front of her, and she refused to miss her chance. Mustering her courage, she picked up the pace and drew near him, squeezing through the crowd, one step, two steps, three—

Until she was right behind him. And touched his robe.[1]

PAIN'S COMPANIONS

Don't you wonder about this poor woman's last decade? What was it like to be her? Mark tells us how she "had suffered much under many physicians, and had spent all that she had, and was no better but rather grew worse" (verse 26). What a terrible compounding effect. The discouraging news, the precious time invested, the money spent . . . on what? On something that made her feel even worse than she did before? Yet I would venture to say this woman had it harder than us for two other reasons.

She was a woman in a man's world, and she was an outcast.

Women and children in Jesus's day were considered of little value. Her social status would have already been affected by this reality—but then, one awful day, her bleeding started. And it wouldn't stop. Jewish purification laws required a menstruating woman to stay away from temple worship (and other people) because she was considered unclean (Leviticus 15:19–31). If her femaleness didn't estrange her enough, her condition sure did. Unwelcome around God's people and unable to do much about it, she likely lost relationships and heart as her health worsened. Scripture doesn't say this in so many words, but I imagine she felt scared and ostracized.

Pain can do this, can't it? Especially when it's chronic and days turn into weeks, then months, then years, and you watch your once-normal life slipping through your fingers. You worry there will be no return. You may have known cerebrally that you weren't in control, but now you *know* you aren't, and that's scary. And when people flock to help you at first but then slowly return to their normal lives, leaving you in your new (awful) normal, and the world doesn't stop just because you're suffering—that compounds the hurt.

Fear and loneliness are two unwelcome companions of pain, and the bleeding woman in Jesus's day likely knew them both. Her story encourages us to ask an important question: Where do we turn for peace when we're in prolonged pain?

TURNING TO CONTROL

Mark highlights how the bleeding woman turned to understanding and answers ("many physicians"), and I would've done the same (Mark 5:26). I *have* done the same. Over six years, I sought the opinions of eight specialty doctors until someone finally diagnosed me with Lyme disease. Each of those visits, though frustrating, was somewhat clarifying, so please don't hear me say that seeking understanding and answers is wrong. We should use every good gift God has given us to seek healing. But I wonder how often we're expecting answers to give us what only God can—a sense of control and the peace that comes with it.

In your pain, in what ways have you tried to take control?

And when it's clear you can't, how do you respond?

Often our pursuit of answers and understanding reveals a deeper desire to manage what feels uncontrollable. "We want to *know* so that we can control," Bobby Jamieson says, "to tame the intolerable unpredictability of how [life] begins and ends."[2] It's unsettling to admit that I'm not actually the master of my own fate, and nothing upends this belief like prolonged pain. The bleeding woman "had suffered much under many physicians," Mark tells us (verse 26), and this reminds us that even the choicest combination of intellect and knowledge can't always make a person whole. Even today, with modern medical advances, doctors are still only practicing medicine. Answers may provide peace of mind, but they can't save a restless soul.

Instead of seeking refuge in answers, where do we turn? The bleeding woman shows us the way. Her impulse was to touch the only One who could make her clean: "She said, 'If I touch even his garments, I will be made well' " (verse 28). Any other human touch would've meant passing her uncleanness to another; only one touch would reverse her curse. Only the Source of life could bring true and lasting healing—not only to her depleted body but also to her languishing soul.

God's promise in our earthly days isn't bodily healing, although perhaps he will grant us that wonderful gift to some degree. His promise is that our faith in Christ will make us well where it matters most—our eternal souls finally at peace, at rest, and healed: "Since we have been justified by faith, we have peace with God through our Lord Jesus Christ" (Romans 5:1). We seek answers, but only one will make a lasting difference: the forgiveness of Jesus, who heals our sin-sickness and brings us back to God. If I have been made better by doctors and have all the answers this world can offer but I don't have God's answer to my greatest problem, I have no actual healing. But one touch from Jesus? Suddenly, my desire for control turns into a desire to trust the One who is in control. And that changes the way I experience pain.

TURNING TO ESCAPE

There's delving into the pain, seeking understanding and answers—and then there's avoiding it. How many of us just want *out* of the pain? If we can't change it, at least we can escape it or numb it for a while. So we try. We convince our weary, discouraged selves that something within our grasp must be worth living for, even if we know the pleasure will fade.

Our modern age offers us unending means of escape from pain. If the hurt won't stop, we can stop the noise in our minds by drowning it in breaking news, social feeds, and streaming services. If we can't deal with our circumstances, we can strike a deal at the office or the gambling table or the retailer. If we don't want to feel the ache, we can experience the pleasure of alcohol or sex or junk food.

Around every corner, escapism invites us to dull the pain. At the heart of our search is a desire for happiness—something to remind us we were made for more than the hardships we face. But this desire eludes us. Just like a person infinitely scrolling on a screen, we're constantly looking for more entertainment, more pleasure, more money, more leisure—and less pain.

But what if, instead of seeking to escape or numb our pain, we listened to it?

And what if it led us into the arms of the One who can strengthen us in it?

The bleeding woman could've stayed in her house, alone and afraid, refusing to confront the condition that had altered her whole life. But "she had heard the reports about Jesus" (Mark 5:27), and those reports gave her more hope than any escapism could. Rather than sitting idle or numbing her pain, she went to see Jesus. She dared to press through the crowd to touch his robe, and she was healed. She took her empty hands and depleted body straight to him and found everything she needed. This is a challenge for us whose hands so often grasp at empty pleasures. As Augustine once said, "God wants to give us something, but cannot, because our hands are full—there's nowhere for Him to put it."[3]

What are you filling your hands with to relieve the pain? What would it look like to open your hands and offer your pain to Jesus? Although he may not heal your body in this earthly life (or may only to a degree), he will fill your hands with greater blessings, and *this* is the hope he gives:

> We rejoice in our sufferings, knowing that suffering produces endurance, and endurance produces character, and character produces hope, and hope does not put us to shame, because God's love has been poured into our hearts through the Holy Spirit who has been given to us. (Romans 5:3–5)

Do we actually believe that God's blessings are better than our idea of blessing, which usually means healing, while his means so much more? Our pain may threaten to put us to shame, but with power and love from Jesus being poured into our hearts, our hope in him will have the final word.

As I've walked through pain, writing has been a way to process and express what Jesus has done within and through me. What about you? How is he calling you to testify to his hope? And what about the woman? Just as she crept up to him under cover of the crowd, he could've healed her quietly, without calling attention to her actions, letting her slip away unannounced. But instead, he called her to testify to his goodness, his healing, his peace. Jesus looked around for her, and "the woman, knowing what had happened to her, came in fear and trembling and fell down before him and told him the whole truth" (Mark 5:33).

Her pain became a platform for his praise.

"Go in peace," Jesus said, "and be healed of your disease" (verse 34).

Because God takes our desperation and touches it with his eternal peace.

WHERE WILL YOU TURN?

Years later, even after finding the right doctor and diagnosis, my pain hasn't stopped. But my restlessness largely has. Jesus is teaching me how to trust him. There is no lasting way to make peace with your pain apart from bringing it to Jesus. So will you? Or will you turn to grasping for control or escaping what you can't control? Neither option will bring you what you're actually looking for—the peace that comes from knowing you'll be okay when you're not okay. And only one person can bring such peace, such sweet relief.

The reports are true. He's right in front of you.

Take hold of Jesus, and he won't ever let you go.

Meeting with Jesus

1. In what ways have you tried to take control of your pain, desperate for a change in circumstances? When it's clear that you can't take control, how do you usually respond?
2. Where do you usually turn to escape from or numb your pain? What would it look like to listen to it instead and let it lead you to Jesus?
3. How does Jesus bring relief through peace with God, even if he doesn't remove your pain in this earthly life? Write out Psalm 40:1–3 and make it your prayer today.

16

When the Miracle Doesn't Come

John 5:5–9

It's been so many years of waiting. Praying. Hoping. Struggling.

I, and all four of our kids suffer from the same devastating disease, something I unknowingly passed on to them at birth. For years, we pursued doctor after doctor, all with differing views on the best path toward healing, only to find ourselves right back where we started. The only things we had to show for it were a waning determination and a dwindling bank account.

Of course, friends, family, and strangers all had their suggestions, even "cure-all" guarantees. But each new proposed solution brought only more discouragement. At times, I felt like resigning myself to our difficult reality. We couldn't keep throwing spaghetti at the wall, hoping it would finally stick.

Long-suffering is often like this. Whether you're praying for healing, longing for a restored marriage, or weighed down by layered sorrows, it's a constant tug-of-war between hope and acceptance. We don't want to stop praying for God's miraculous hand and pursuing change with the resources he provides. But in our humanity, we grow weary, discouraged, and unsure if healing or change will ever happen.

For many years, I struggled with shame over this yo-yo effect of long-suffering. I would set out with new resolve to pray with great expectation, believing that God *can and does* still do miracles. But as time went on and I didn't see the change I hoped for, my prayers lessened. I admit, it can be tempting to cease praying altogether when God's answers don't meet my expectations, rather than submitting my expectations to the truth that God's infinite mind understands things that my finite mind simply can't. Therefore, when he doesn't grant me what I desperately desire, it can be a struggle to hold both hope and acceptance in faithful tension.

Can you relate?

Even more, as followers of Jesus, we can be tempted to question God's goodness and love for us in the waiting. If God can heal me and my kids, rescue me from the sorrows of this world, and grant my desires, why doesn't he? The flame of doubt is further fanned when I see others receive the miracle I desire. *Is there something wrong with me? What are they doing right that I'm missing?*

These doubts are some of the most damaging arrows in the enemy's arsenal. Because if we question God's goodness and love, the very foundation we stand on becomes quicksand beneath our spiritual feet. As we sink further into our doubts, belief about who God is can falter—founded no longer on his Word but on the ebb and flow of our perception. And if we aren't careful, cynicism and a hardness of heart can slowly pull us further into independence and bitter resentment toward the God we believe let us down.

May this never be the case! To guard ourselves from it, we have to first recognize the sinking sand of unchecked doubt. Thankfully, Jesus hasn't left us to ourselves to navigate the difficult road of long-suffering.

LEARNING FROM JESUS

This week, I was freshly struck by the account of Jesus healing a man who had been an invalid for thirty-eight years as he lay helplessly in front of the pool of Bethesda. John tells the story:

> When Jesus saw him lying there and knew that he had already been there a long time, he said to him, "Do you want to be healed?" The sick man answered him, "Sir, I have no one to put me into the pool when the water is stirred up, and while I am going another steps down before me." Jesus said to him, "Get up, take up your bed, and walk." And at once the man was healed, and he took up his bed and walked. (John 5:6–9)

Jesus already knew this man's story. And he knew this man's heart. We don't know why he zeroed in on this particular man, when many others were hurting around him, but the Scriptures specify that Jesus knew the length of time he had suffered—and had compassion toward the longevity of his suffering. Jesus knew every detail of this man's life. The man had nothing impressive to show for himself, nothing to offer, and no value according to the world's standards. Yet Jesus pursued him. And the same is true for you.

He sees you, even when no one else does. He knows the length and layers of your suffering and the weariness it has brought.

And more than anything else—he draws near and calls you by name.

Interestingly, Jesus didn't ask the man if he believed he was the Son of God. He didn't immediately ask him to repent of his sin. He simply asked, "Do you want to be healed?" (verse 6).

At first glance, I thought, *Of course he wants to be healed. What kind of question is that? Everyone wants to be healed.* But I wonder, after the man had spent so many years as an invalid, perhaps Jesus was asking, "Do you believe you *can* be healed? Or have you sealed your fate, closed your heart, and given up hope?"

That question convicts me. It's easy to grow hardened by years of long-suffering. As much as we hate our pain, it can subtly become our identity when we've lived with it for so long. If it's all we know, it can become all we see of ourselves (and we expect others to treat us accordingly). Even more, it can taint the way we view God and the world around us.

But as we've seen all throughout the previous chapters, Jesus is so patient with us. In the Gospels, he often drew the heart of a person to the surface by asking a question, rather than giving a command or beelining toward repentance. And in this instance, he asked a question that began to draw to the surface where this man was placing his hope.

FOCUSING ON THE CHALLENGES

I chuckled when I first read the man's response to Jesus's question. Not because it's innately funny, but because we're so limited by our human understanding, despite having direct access to the God of the universe. The man seems to have responded to Jesus's question as if Jesus were saying something else: "If you really want to be healed, then why don't you do more? If you really want to be healed, why don't you get into the medicinal pool and *help yourself*?"

Perhaps, like today, this was a common self-help narrative.

But this man was standing before his Creator, the very One who spoke the world into existence and could bring the dead to life, yet all he could see were hindrances to healing.

How often do we do the same? We become so focused on all we're up against that we lose sight of the One who rules over every single molecule and atom, along with every circumstance we deem impossible.

But, friend, there are also deeper questions to ask ourselves: Do we truly want to be made more like Jesus, even if at the cost of earthly comfort? Can we trust that he might have good for us beyond what we perceive? These are not easy questions to answer, because they go against our longing for relief now.

Therefore, it's important to examine what our belief in God's goodness is founded on. Is it based on the fact that he's granted (or not granted) what seems good in *our* eyes? Or is it based on his promise of good to us, which sometimes comes in unwanted packages?

If it's the first, we'll question his goodness every time his will collides with ours. If it's the second, we'll learn to remain hopeful while anchoring ourselves to the character and promises of God.

UNMERITED GRACE, UNDESERVED MIRACLES

Jesus didn't scold the man for his shortsighted answer. He graciously healed him anyway. The man didn't deserve it. He didn't earn it. He didn't pray the right prayer. He wasn't of more value than those around him. He was simply a recipient of grace to display God's life-changing power.

And that's true for each of us. Sometimes God shows his power by healing us, providing a much-needed job, fulfilling our longings, or granting a miracle. And if he does, it's not because of our own merit. But sometimes (or most of the time), he shows his power by sustaining us through the impossible, giving us joy in the midst of sorrow, and changing us instead of our circumstances.

I think of Joni Eareckson Tada, who was paralyzed in a diving accident at the age of seventeen. Because of God's redeeming purposes, her life has become a beacon of hope to countless people through a worldwide disability ministry born out of circumstances that, at the time, seemed void of any possible good.

I think of Betsie and Corrie ten Boom, whose courage and faith drove them to risk their lives to save persecuted Jewish people during the Holocaust. Although they lost so much in the process (including Betsie's own life), their profound faith in Jesus amid the stench of death and evil wasn't wasted. Not only did they share the hope of Jesus with women in their barracks; they also personally experienced the depths of Jesus's presence in the deepest pit. When Betsie neared death's door, she whispered to Corrie, "[We] must tell people what we have learned here. We must tell them that there is no pit so deep that He is not deeper still. They will listen to us, Corrie, because we have been here."[1] Corrie went on to encourage countless lives for years to come, showing God's love and grace against the backdrop of a dark and evil world.

God is often providing miracles of grace in ongoing suffering. We just need the eyes to see them.

JESUS'S MIRACLES ARE MEANT TO GIVE US MORE OF HIM

Interestingly, in John 5, at first glance it seems like the invalid's interaction with Jesus ended when Jesus physically healed him and let him go on his way. But if you read farther, a little while later Jesus found this man again in the temple and revealed his need for salvation from sin, not just sickness.

Jesus said, "See, you are well! Sin no more, that nothing worse may happen to you" (verse 14). There's some debate on what Jesus meant by "that nothing worse may happen to you," but we can assume that, in part, he meant spiritual healing was of even greater value than physical. Why? Because Jesus knows that eternal separation from God is a far greater kind of suffering.

Friend, if God hasn't granted you the longings of your heart, rest in this: If you are a follower of Jesus, you *are* a miracle of God's grace (Ephesians 2:8–9). Jesus chose not to use his power to heal, protect, and rescue himself when faced with the agony of the cross so that *you* could be healed, protected, and rescued eternally—no matter what this life brings. As followers of Jesus, we, too, are called to walk in the footsteps of our suffering (but victorious) Savior.

Yes, God may grant earthly relief from your suffering, but he will always offer you himself regardless of the circumstances (2 Corinthians 1:3–7). As you pray and wait with hopeful expectation of his goodness, he promises to provide all you need to live the life he's called you to live.

Today let's pray with hope and acceptance. Let's rest assured that God loves us with the tender love of a Father who knows what's best for us and will bring it about in his perfect timing. We may walk with wounds that we long to be healed from and scars that bear evidence to the pain we've endured, but because Jesus willingly endured the wounds of this world and bore the scars of our sins, we can press on in this hope:

> I heard a loud voice from the throne saying, "Behold, the dwelling place of God is with man. He will dwell with them, and they will be his people, and God himself will be with them as their God. He will wipe away every tear from their eyes, and death shall be no more, neither shall there be mourning, nor crying, nor pain anymore, for the former things have passed away."
>
> And he who was seated on the throne said, "Behold, I am making all things new." (Revelation 21:3–5)

Meeting with Jesus

1. Do you believe God can still do miracles in your life? Why or why not?
2. Recall a time when God didn't change your circumstances but changed you through those circumstances. In what ways did you feel tempted to doubt and question, and how did God use that time to grow you?
3. What trial are you facing today that you can apply these truths to as you continue to pray for relief? Read and write out Psalm 23, then journal these verses into your own prayer as you wait on God for the answers you long for.

17

When You Wonder If God's Punishing You

John 9:1–12

Suffering. Nobody wants it. And rarely can we make sense of it.

That's why, when life hurts, we often look for someone or something to blame. Something is awry, and our pain needs somewhere to go.

At times, there's an easy target for our blame. Someone ran a red light, and their negligence is now the cause of our debilitating back pain; a friend spread a false accusation against us, and we're left to pick up the pieces of our reputation; a doctor's error turned a routine surgery into the heart-wrenching loss of our loved one.

But that logic has nowhere to go when a diagnosis shatters our once-comfortable life or a tornado rips through our town, taking the life we knew right along with it.

Most often, we turn in one of two directions: We blame God, whom we trusted to protect us from such senseless heartbreak, or we blame ourselves, convinced we must have done something to deserve such pain.

Believe it or not, people have used the same logic for ages.

CAUSE AND EFFECT

Like many of us, the disciples wanted to make sense of the suffering they saw. Therefore, when they came across a blind beggar in John 9, they boldly asked Jesus, "Rabbi, who sinned, this man or his parents, that he was born blind?" (verse 2). In their eyes, there was no third option. Someone was to blame.

Let the implications of this sink in for a moment. The disciples weren't trying to be cruel by questioning this poor man and his parents. It simply exposes our human tendency to try to make sense of what seems senseless. After all, if we can pinpoint the cause, maybe we can prevent that same hardship from coming to us.

Have you been on the receiving end of this logic? It can sound something like this:

> "Have you asked God to reveal the unconfessed sin that's at the root of your suffering?"
>
> "Have you figured out where you went wrong for this to have occurred?"
>
> "Is there a generational sin that has yet to be confronted and confessed?"
>
> "I bet ______ is the reason God allowed this to happen."

Sometimes those accusations and assumptions come from others, and sometimes they come from within our own troubled hearts. Either way, they stem from the belief that we should have complete control over (or at least know the cause of) our circumstances.

Of course, at times we suffer the natural consequences of our choices. If I'm dishonest with those around me, I'll suffer broken relationships because I've proved to be untrustworthy. If I choose laziness and gluttony over taking care of the body God's given me, I may suffer the natural consequences of health complications. If I make unwise financial decisions, I may fall into debt.

However, much of the suffering we endure is simply part of living in a fallen world groaning under the curse of sin, death, and decay. We can't control the genetics we were born with, the stock market crash, the drunk driver who careened across three lanes, the flash flood that even weather radar systems didn't see coming, or the countless other challenges that come at us without notice. No, most of the suffering in this world contains mysteries that God alone knows. It's prideful to believe we have more control over our circumstances than we really do.

Thankfully, Jesus doesn't leave us to our floundering selves.

HE HAS A GREATER VISION TO GIVE US

Jesus confronted the disciples' distorted belief system: "It was not that this man sinned, or his parents, but that the works of God might be displayed in him" (John 9:3).

This poor blind beggar had suffered greatly throughout his life. We don't know if he heard the disciples' question to Jesus or not, but here's what we do know: Jesus immediately defended him. Had this man sinned? Of course he had. And so had his parents. But Jesus clarified this wasn't the *cause* of his suffering. Not only did Jesus challenge their simplistic view of suffering and ultimately point them to the greater purpose of his glory; he also fiercely defended a helpless man. Jesus was like a father stepping in front of a child: "To get to him, you'll first have to go through me."

What a Savior we have—forgiver of the sinner, helper of the helpless, defender of the defenseless. Yes, he came to expose the darkness of hearts, but he also came to shine the light of his hope and glory into the dark places of our pain (verse 5). It's tempting to assume God looks at our pain and wonders, *Why are you struggling? Don't you see that I'm doing something through it?*

But Jesus's heart is empathetic, not critical.

The comforting truth is that he doesn't use our pain by sacrificing our good on the altar of his glory. Even though he knew his plan of redemption, Jesus's life on earth shows us how much he still empathizes and grieves with us over the brokenness of the world. And everything he does brings him the greatest glory *and* us the greatest good (Romans 8:28). If we question that truth, we'll constantly question his heart for us when we can't understand his ways. But Psalm 56 assures us, "This I know, that God is for me" (verse 9). Our faith will be bolstered when it's founded on the knowledge that God is undeniably, without a doubt, *for us*.

Like Jesus, we can acknowledge pain for what it is. But even when it all *feels* pointless, we know our story isn't finished. Jesus simply asks us to trust him as we endure in the waiting.

WHAT'S THE POINT?

Jesus sees everything from a multidimensional viewpoint, whereas we see only from a one-dimensional perspective. Even more than our temporary comfort, Jesus desires to partner with us in displaying his goodness and glory. He does this for our deepest joy *and* to awaken the hearts of those around us.

But before he can work *through* us, he must work *in* us. As Paul Tripp says, "God often uses the hardest things in life to produce the best things in us. . . . God often compromises our comfort in order to produce something even better in us: godly character."[1] Although we'd be satisfied with quick relief, Jesus has so much more to give us than momentary happiness. Because of that, he sometimes allows the temporary pain of our suffering (the very thing we may assume is a punishment or sign of his displeasure) to chisel away our rough earthly edges to shape us more into his image. And I say this as one who's experienced it firsthand.

Several years ago, my family went through a painful season of financial whiplash. My husband's intense on-call job (which he'd done successfully for ten years) was no longer sustainable with our family's declining health and the destructive nature of our son's challenges. In a step of sacrificial faith, my husband changed careers, taking a massive pay cut in the process. Not long after, the new company began to struggle in a declining economy and my husband was out of a job. In a matter of eighteen months, we went from living in the home of our dreams to joblessness, downsizing to a rental home with an unknown infestation of fleas, and living on food stamps.

Let's just say, my initial response to our circumstances wasn't one of my finest moments. It felt like God had pulled the rug out from under us after we'd tried to honor him by prioritizing the health and unity of our family over a comfortable lifestyle. Instead of obedience leading to blessing, it seemed to bring only loss.

I won't go into detail, but God used that long, painful season to strip away many earthly comforts (and my pride along with them), gradually opening my eyes to what I needed more than a life of ease: to be content with less and grateful for things I once glossed over and to evaluate what I worshipped more—God or the blessings he gives. It was a painful season beyond what words can express. But it's also a season I'm now truly grateful for. God took a lot from me, but he gave me so much more in its place.

Friend, your suffering isn't God's punishment, and it's never pointless. Jesus is always at work in ways we can't see in the moment. And it's always for the purpose of showing the goodness and glory of God to us, in us, and through us.

"WHY" NEVER SATISFIES

Still, we think, *If I just knew why, then I could endure.* But what we ultimately need more than anything else is not the light that shines on the answers we want but the light of Jesus himself (John 9:5). Jesus could have explained the man's blindness, but he didn't. That wasn't what the man *really* needed. Yes, it would have been God's undeserved grace to spare him from a gene mutation, disease, or whatever caused his blindness. His life would have been easier. Had that been the case, though, would he have come face-to-face with Jesus? Maybe not. He would have been content with his physical sight, despite walking in spiritual darkness. But in the hands of a powerful God, it was also an undeserved grace for the blind beggar's life to become a remarkable story of redemption that led him (and those around him) to spiritual sight.

You may not see it now, but answers to your pain won't bring ultimate comfort. Only nearness to Jesus will. Jesus wants what is best for you and has the power to bring it about. More than anything else, John reminds us that it is only the light of Christ that will illuminate these dark days. Not always in a way that makes sense of them, but in a way that leads us to see that his presence and comfort in our pain are greater gifts than the answers we seek.

Jesus may not tell you why you lost your job, but he'll show you how personal of a God he is as he provides for specific needs that only he knows exist. Jesus may not tell you why your cancer has returned, but he'll infuse you with God-sized courage, comfort, and strength one moment at a time. When Jesus is near, the need to know why fades into the background.

PAIN IN THE HANDS OF A REDEEMER

Now if we continue reading, John does recount Jesus's healing of this man's blindness. Interestingly, he didn't simply command his sight to return. Instead, he mixed mud with his saliva, spread it over his eyes (eww), and instructed him to go wash in the pool of Siloam.

We can't overlook the deeper meaning here.

God wants to involve us in the process of his work in us. He wants a personal relationship with us, not just a transactional one. I wonder at times if that's why it's actually his grace to *not* immediately bring us the answers or relief we want. He knows our hearts are prone to wander. He knows when relief would deprive us of our greatest need. As Paul Tripp goes on to say, "His plan is not just to forgive us, but also to refine us by his grace. . . . He refines us so that the only explanation for the way we live is that we have been touched by the power of his refining grace."[2]

Redemption isn't found only on the other side of the pain. It's experienced moment by moment as we long for the help and nearness of Jesus even more than we long for relief. Little by little, he offers us the healing ointment of his truth, then asks us to step out in faith, trusting that his truth will always leave us changed.

THE RIPPLE EFFECTS OF GLORY

Somehow, as he works *in* us, his light begins to shine *through* us. The beggar followed Jesus's instructions in faith, and immediately his sight was restored. Naturally, he quickly became the talk of the town. Many who had previously seen him in the streets began to wonder, "Isn't this the one who used to sit begging?" (John 9:8, CSB). When he confirmed their suspicions, they asked, "Then how were your eyes opened?" (verse 10). He replied that Jesus had healed him. This beggar's healing was a gift of grace, not only because his suffering ended, but also because he had the privilege of partnering with Jesus in the mission of pointing others to his sight-giving power (not only physically but also spiritually).

Friend, our suffering—whether it displays God's power to save or shows God's power to sustain—is about far more than us. God wants to redeem our suffering not only twofold, but tenfold, a hundredfold, and far beyond what we may ever see in our lifetime. If we grasp this, our suffering won't feel pointless.

In fact, some of the most powerful ripple effects of God's glory through the lives of his suffering saints haven't come through a miraculous change in circumstances. Instead, they've come as others stand in awe of a sufferer who is faithfully enduring with a strength beyond human means and wonder, *Who is this Jesus who brings such comfort?*

As Charles Spurgeon once said, "My dear friend, sometimes God works a greater wonder when he sustains people in trouble than by delivering them. To let the bush burn with fire and not be consumed is a greater thing than quenching the flame and saving the bush."[3]

God could display his miraculous power by changing our circumstances in one fell swoop, making others stop and wonder for a time, *Who is this God who does such miracles?* But when others around us (both Christians and non-Christians) see us enduring in suffering because Jesus is a greater treasure than the relief we desire, it continuously puts God's power, glory, and worth on display to all those who are watching.

As my wise friend Vaneetha Risner once said to me, "When we see [someone] who seems to have everything going for them, we want their life. But when we see someone being upheld and sustained in brokenness, we want their God."

Those words have stuck with me. I'm pretty sure nobody wants my life—but I do hope that by watching my life, they will want my God.

My fellow sufferer, if you have heard the whispers that you are to blame for your hardships but you see no clear correlations between sin and its natural consequences, take heart. Your suffering isn't reduced to the effect of your choices. Jesus tells us clearly in John 16:33, "I have told you these things, so that in me you may have peace. In this world you will have trouble. But take heart! I have overcome the world" (NIV). You and I will have trouble in this world because it groans to be made new. We may not be able to make sense of the why behind our circumstances, but we are not left without hope. We can face the difficult days ahead with the peace that

Jesus gives, knowing his redeeming power will have the final word. He has overcome the world, and if we are his followers, then we, too, will be overcomers.

And he has declared, "The one who overcomes, I will grant to him to sit with Me on My throne, as I also overcame and sat with My Father on His throne" (Revelation 3:21, NASB).

Oh, what a day that will be!

Meeting with Jesus

1. How do you think about the reasons for your suffering (consequences of sin, effects of the Fall, etc.)? Where did that perspective come from?
2. To what degree do you think we have control over the circumstances that come into our lives? Is your answer based on what the Bible says or on your experiences? Read James 4:13–15 and Proverbs 19:21.
3. Write down a specific circumstance you are facing right now. What grief, heartache, limitations, or questions has it caused? Acknowledge those things to God. Now write a prayer to offer that circumstance to the Lord.

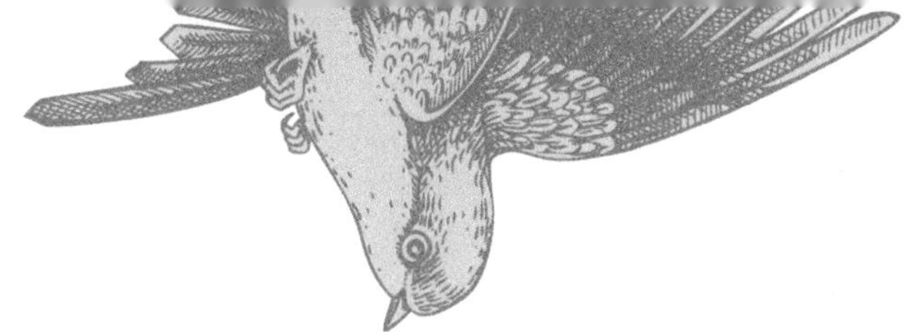

PART 5

DOUBT

18

When You Feel Like a Bad Christian

Mark 9:20–24

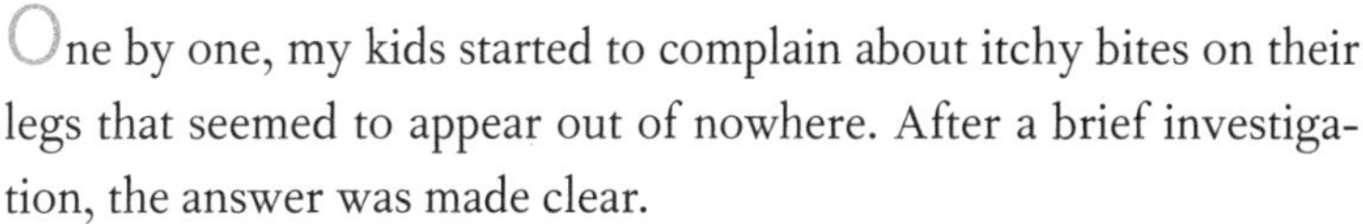

One by one, my kids started to complain about itchy bites on their legs that seemed to appear out of nowhere. After a brief investigation, the answer was made clear.

Our rental home was infested with fleas. Yes, fleas.

It was determined that, despite the fact that we had no pets of our own, our backyard was the neighborhood highway for rodents, bringing a steady supply of fleas onto our property. By the time it was discovered, the whole house was infested.

Honestly, I wanted to run for the hills and never look back. I was sicker than ever before, and all four of our children had been recently diagnosed with a disease that I had unknowingly passed on. We were enduring extreme challenges with our neurodivergent child. I was struggling to walk as a decades-old ankle injury made mobility increasingly difficult. And to make matters worse, my husband had just lost his job in company-wide layoffs during a time when our medical expenses were piling up. No part of us seemed untouched by trouble.

As if I had a stress fracture in my soul, I was convinced one more blow would break me beyond repair. And the flea infestation felt, to me, like that final blow.

Needless to say, doubts, questions, and anger quickly followed.

Why, God? Where is your compassion in this? I want to believe you care, but this feels cruel.

Those words felt faithless and so very wrong. But pretending they didn't exist would only push me further away from the Lord. I could no longer deny the questions and doubts that plagued me. I desperately wanted to trust him, to believe in all the promises I had staked my life on. But hope felt like a setup for disappointment.

Have you felt this? Have you been afraid to admit those feelings exist?

WHEN EXPERIENCE CLOUDS OUR FAITH

Thankfully, the Bible makes it clear that we aren't the first ones to experience doubts when circumstances leave our faith hanging by a thread. In the Old Testament, it's sobering to read the accusations of Job and Jeremiah. However, God clearly saw fit to include them in Scripture, bearing witness to the spiritual wrestling we all face.

In Mark's gospel, we come across yet another example.

A desperate father longed for his son to be free from the lifelong torment of a demon but struggled to believe it could be done. His son, who was likely a teenager or older, had been plagued by this demon since childhood. Not only did this man suffer the horrifying reality of a demon tormenting his child, he was also helpless to do anything about it. I can't imagine the anguish he faced.

But just when all hope seemed lost, he received word that Jesus and his disciples were in town performing miracles—even casting out demons. Could he believe his ears? I imagine a hope arose that he dared not feel again. Maybe, just maybe, his hopes for his son would finally be realized.

As he saw miracle after miracle performed by the disciples, his confidence must have grown by the moment. Suddenly, he stood before them as his son cautiously stepped forward. The disciples ordered the evil spirit to be cast out in the power of Jesus—only to find their words powerless.

Hopeless. Again.

Even worse, an argument now arose between the religious leaders and the disciples, who were confused by their sudden lack of miraculous power. After all, they had cast out countless other demons. Why not this one too?

This poor father. I empathize deeply with him. Can't you?

If I were in his shoes, doubt, embarrassment, disappointment, confusion, and despair would have descended on me with a vengeance. In my own way, I've been there. Disappointed that Jesus wasn't acting in my life how I thought he would. Confused over why he answered others' prayers so powerfully yet seemed silent to mine. *Did I do something wrong? Am I too weak in faith?* Worst of all—*how do I believe in the love, goodness, and power of Jesus when experience seems to say otherwise?*

If God's promises are true, what do we do with our questions and doubts when he acts counter to everything that makes sense to us?

Maybe you prayed for protection from harm, only to hear, "You have cancer."

Maybe you pleaded for a child's healing, only to attend their funeral weeks later.

Maybe you worked with integrity, only to find yourself unemployed with a dwindling bank account.

Maybe you prayed for freedom from the darkness of depression, only to find its grip tightening all the more.

Like this father, we all find ourselves facing circumstances that cloak the God we thought we knew in a cloud of mystery. We wouldn't be human if these moments didn't leave us confused and shaken. If our earthly father told us that he'd love and protect us at all costs but then stood idly by when we found ourselves in danger, we'd rightly question his faithfulness.

That logic seems natural to us. Our brains are wired to learn from experience. Therefore, as we mentioned earlier, it's easy to say we believe God is good and faithful when life goes well. But that belief is tested when our idea of good doesn't line up with the circumstances God has allowed.

How, then, are we to view these unsettling seasons of doubt? Pretend they don't exist? Fake a smile on Sunday while seeds of resentment silently take root during the week? Or do we face them head-on?

The rest of this passage gives us a starting point.

DOUBT ISN'T THE SAME AS UNBELIEF

Jesus arrived on the scene to find his disciples arguing with the religious leaders. The father spoke up:

> "Teacher, I brought my son to you, for he has a spirit that makes him mute. And whenever it seizes him, it throws him down, and he foams and grinds his teeth and becomes rigid. So I asked your disciples to cast it out, and they were not able." And he answered them, "O faithless generation, how long am I to be with you? How long am I to bear with you? Bring him to me." (Mark 9:17–19)

When I first read Jesus's response, I was confused by it. I thought he was calling out the father's unbelief here, but actually, it was the disciples'. The disciples were commissioned to heal and cast out demons by relying on the power of Jesus, not themselves. He was calling them out for their lack of dependence on the Holy Spirit to do the work through prayer.

It's important to note, then, that faith *does* matter—not necessarily the strength of our faith, but the source of our faith. It's natural for us to rely on our human perspective, often equating a positive or negative outcome with evidence for or against God's favor toward us. But Jesus reminds us that our faith isn't rooted in what we can control, what we believe is best, or what makes sense from our limited vantage point. Our faith must be rooted in who Jesus says he is, even when the outcome is uncertain or his ways perplex us. Sometimes *not* receiving the outcome we desire reveals where our faith really resides. Other times it forces our shallow faith to grow deeper as the winds of doubt threaten to uproot it.

The truth is, doubt isn't the opposite of faith. Unbelief is. Doubt says, "I want to believe, but I'm struggling." Unbelief says, "What I once believed isn't true," so we walk away with hardened hearts that are unwilling to surrender to the Lord's ways.

Perhaps you've felt guilt and shame for battling thoughts of doubt. Let's challenge that way of thinking. What if doubt isn't a threat to our faith—what if it's an opportunity? What if doubt breaks down weak faith muscles, ultimately making us stronger in the Lord?

Consider what happens when our bodies are pushed beyond their comfort zones. Muscles experience small tears that, in the short term, cause pain and greater weakness. At the moment, we feel worse off than before. But we push ourselves anyway, don't we? Why? Because we know that our muscles have to be stretched beyond what they can currently bear to grow stronger.

Similarly, if our faith is never stretched—if we never experience little pains of doubt—we will have no reason to draw nearer to Jesus. We won't go deeper into his Word in search of answers or end up with a stronger, enduring faith. So, dear reader, your doubts aren't a threat to your faith; they're an opportunity to be strengthened. After all, your faith was never about your strength or worthiness but about Jesus's strength and faithfulness to hold on to you.

And that is precisely where we see Jesus lead this father's heart in Mark 9:

> They brought the boy to him. And when the spirit saw him, immediately it convulsed the boy, and he fell on the ground and rolled about, foaming at the mouth. And Jesus asked his father, "How long has this been happening to him?" And he said, "From childhood. And it has often cast him into fire and into water, to destroy him. But if you can do anything, have compassion on us and help us." And Jesus said to him, "'If you can'! All things are possible for one who believes." Immediately the father of the child cried out and said, "I believe; help my unbelief!" (verses 20–24)

HELP MY UNBELIEF

Understandably, the father now approached Jesus with a shaky faith. He couldn't endure more heartbreak. But he mustered the courage to answer Jesus directly, despite the doubts plaguing him.

Jesus's response? He both received his struggling faith and called him to greater faith at the same time.

It's important to distinguish between what Jesus was saying and what he was *not* saying here. He wasn't saying that everything asked for is a *guarantee* for the one who believes; he was saying that all things are *possible*. Your faith doesn't guarantee the outcome you desire.

Just as he called this father, Jesus calls us to greater faith in him as the satisfier of our deepest desires. Not because he requires perfect faith in order to receive us, but because he knows unshakable, resilient faith in him will bring a comfort and strength beyond any earthly gift he could give us.

So, as I have gradually learned in my own long seasons of wrestling with the mysterious ways of my Lord, I can come to him honestly, not pretending my doubts don't exist, but simply praying, "I believe; help my unbelief!"

I still loathe the existence of fleas, but those loathsome pests that once drove my heart to question the love and goodness of God gradually became a reminder that even when my faith is shaken, Jesus is faithful. He never promised freedom from suffering in this broken world. But he promises to provide strength equal to the need.

Friend, Jesus is willing to receive your wounded, weak, and shaken faith. He won't condemn you; he'll strengthen you. This is the only remedy for a fractured faith, and he alone offers it to you.

Today, rather than running from your doubts, run straight into the gracious, strong arms of Jesus. He will not turn away a heart in need.

Meeting with Jesus

1. What detail or encouragement stands out most in this story or chapter? Why is that?
2. How have your doubts deepened your faith? If you can't confidently say they have, take a moment and pray this simple prayer: "I believe, but, Lord, help my unbelief."
3. Read James 1:5–6. Journal about specific doubts you have today, trusting he already knows and has the strength and wisdom you need.

19

When You Fear Your Faith Will Fail

Luke 22:31–34

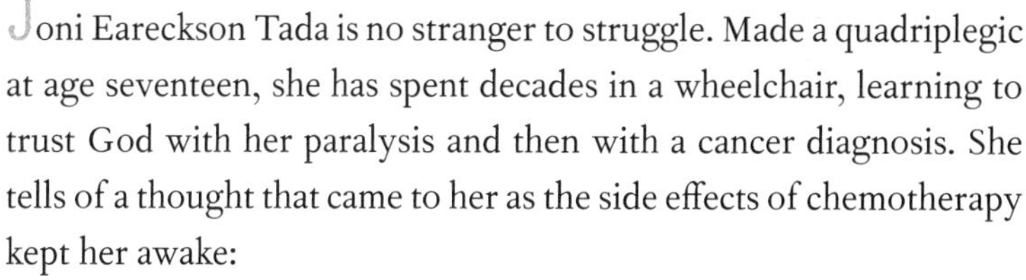

Joni Eareckson Tada is no stranger to struggle. Made a quadriplegic at age seventeen, she has spent decades in a wheelchair, learning to trust God with her paralysis and then with a cancer diagnosis. She tells of a thought that came to her as the side effects of chemotherapy kept her awake:

> I remember something dynamic and electrifying is abuzz in my dark room. The unseen world in the spirit realm, all the heavenly hosts, including powers and principalities, they're watching me. They're listening to me. And as I respond, they are learning about God and His character through me. . . .
>
> God's reputation is on the line. . . . When the spirit world sees God's strong arms uphold you in your weakness, the Father gets the glory.[1]

How often do you consider the spiritual realm? How aware are you of the invisible cosmic activity happening around you? Maybe

Tada's comments catch you off guard, and understandably so. These are stretching, disquieting thoughts, but we must consider them. We struggle not just with things in our ordinary earthly existence—bank accounts and relationships and crazy schedules and crazier children and natural disasters and cancer and big questions about God—but with things beyond this realm. The Bible tells us there are spiritual beings, both good and evil, all around us: "spiritual forces of evil" who despise God (Ephesians 6:12) as well as heavenly hosts who serve him in allegiance and love (Job 38:5–7; Psalm 89:5–7; Hebrews 1:14).

A divine drama is taking place all around us.

Recognizing it is the only way we will deal adequately with our doubts.

Opposing our journey to heaven is the same serpent who unleashed sin into the world, so we don't take him lightly. "The world is a snare to the believer," Ryle writes. "The flesh is a burden and a clog. But there is no enemy so dangerous as that restless, invisible, experienced enemy, the devil."[2]

We turn now to Peter because Jesus wanted him awake to the divine drama surrounding him, and Jesus wants us awake too. As we struggle with doubt, we need to know *we're in a war.* Facing our doubts, fighting them, confronting them—however you want to phrase it—we're dealing not with fantasy but with significant spiritual forces, and our faith in Jesus Christ is at stake.

CHARACTER 1: THE SIFTER

Luke's account of this divine drama involves three important characters: the Sifter, the Intercessor, and the Strengthener. When Jesus turned to Peter, the men were sitting around a table, surrounded by the other disciples. They had just eaten the Passover meal and the very first Lord's Supper. Jesus said to Peter,

> "Simon, Simon, behold, Satan demanded to have you, that he might sift you like wheat, but I have prayed for you that your faith may not fail. And when you have turned again, strengthen your brothers." Peter said to him, "Lord, I am ready to go with you both to prison and to death." Jesus said, "I tell you, Peter, the rooster will not crow this day, until you deny three times that you know me." (Luke 22:31–34)

Satan, in the heavenly courtroom, had made his demand. He wanted Peter. Which sounds terribly discouraging—but his demand should actually encourage us. Why? *Because Satan submits to God.* He can't do whatever he wants; Jesus and Satan aren't two equal gods vying for power. There is only one all-powerful, victorious God, and "Satan must go to [him] for permission before he can trouble the lives of God's children," John Piper says.[3]

What is our enemy's goal? Above all, he wants to destroy our trust in Jesus. He wants to sift us like wheat, shaking us around temptation's sieve until we slip through, down to his domain of unbelief. What will that take? He may bring suffering and pain, loss and grief. Or he may use prosperity and ease, delusion and apathy. Whatever tactics he uses, his aim is to ruin your faith.

Friend, your enemy is real and his ambitions are wicked. The doubts you're facing today, whether world-upending or small and creeping, are a breeding ground for his terrible work. Our awareness of this should bolster us rather than discourage us. *We know what he's up to. We are not ignorant*. No one can successfully fight an unknown enemy—but as for ours, we are well aware of his slimy schemes (2 Corinthians 2:11; Ephesians 6:11). And this means we can actually call him out, with all the strength our God supplies.

He may want to sift us like wheat—but Jesus wants us more.

And what Jesus wants, Jesus gets.

CHARACTER 2: THE INTERCESSOR

What if you could hear Jesus praying for you in the next room? As I've walked through seasons of doubt and discouragement, this thought has buoyed me. *My friend, my Lord, my advocate, is praying for me. Right now.* So far in this book, we've talked a lot about what Jesus has already done for us, but how about what he's currently doing? Our answer matters. It's hard to trust someone if we don't know where they went or what they're up to. Confidence comes from clarity, and Peter's conversation with Jesus gives us a clue: "I have prayed for you" (Luke 22:32). *Jesus is praying for you right now in heaven.* If you belong to him and are one of God's own people, then you can know that Jesus is actively talking to his Father on your behalf.

He's strengthening your faith in him.

He's making sure you make it to glory.

If your enemy's goal is to destroy your trust in God, then Jesus's goal is to fortify it. He does this in many ways, namely through means of grace. He speaks to you in Scripture, listens to you in prayer, and ministers to you through the church and sacraments (like baptism and the Lord's Supper). But do we consider that he also strengthens us by *praying* for us? How incredibly personal and deeply touching—that God Almighty is praying for you and me. Just like Old Testament priests would talk to God on behalf of the people, Jesus is talking to God on your behalf *right now.* This means all the more because he knows your frame; he knows what it means to be human; he knows what it's like to be you. His prayers for you are deeply empathetic.

He is your faithful and mighty intercessor.

Have you ever had someone intercede for you in an extra special way? One of my elderly friends from church is gifted in intercessory prayer, and when she prays for me, I feel strengthened to endure. How much more when Jesus prays for us?

John 17 is one long prayer straight from Jesus's mouth that gives us insight into how he prays. He said, "Holy Father, keep them in your name, which you have given me. . . . I do not ask that you take them out of the world, but that you keep them from the evil one" (verses 11, 15). *Jesus prays that you will be safe from Satan and saved for God*, that your soul will belong to him no matter what befalls you.

Now, does this mean you will never be tempted or stumble or sin? Of course not. Even in praying for Peter, Jesus knew the disciple would deny him three times—and he did. While Jesus's prayers can certainly protect us from sin, they don't perfect us from sin on earth (Romans 7:22–23; Jude 24). But his prayers ensure our heavenly security. Those who belong to God can't be taken from his fierce embrace, no matter how fierce the onslaught may feel. "I give [you] eternal life," Jesus said, "and [you] will never perish, and no one will snatch [you] out of my hand" (John 10:28). That's a comforting promise for easily tempted, unfaithful people like us.

I have prayed for you that your faith may not fail.

But what if it seems like our faith has failed? What if, like Peter, we have believed our enemy's lies and capitulated? What if our doubts have been overwhelmingly strong, our eyes have beheld unholy images, our fears have propelled foolish decisions, and our mouths and hands have disobeyed our Lord? What then?

We look to the promise of redemption: Because of Jesus's prayers, what Satan uses to derail our faith will serve only to strengthen it—and the faith of those around us.

CHARACTER 3: THE STRENGTHENER

I gazed around the room at the group of women gathered before me, and I hesitated to speak. How could I, the pastor's wife, possibly share about the doubts I'd been having? Wouldn't this discourage my small group? Wasn't I supposed to be an example, someone to encourage them rather than need encouragement from them?

But this was precisely the lie my accuser wanted me to believe.

A lie to shame me into silence.

Yet God's truth broke through that afternoon, and I believe Jesus's prayers urged me onward to a place of honesty and humility. I was a weak person with a strong Savior, and he knew how badly I needed his church body to strengthen me. So I shared—with tears and trepidation. And when I did, something happened. A weight rose from my embarrassed shoulders, and I was given the easy and light yoke of his love. I was surrounded by women who not only appreciated my confession but also said, "Me too." Far from being alone in my doubts and spiritual questions, I had sisters who understood and prayed for me.

God's grace does this. He uses Satan's ploys to advance his purposes instead, turning evil on its head and strengthening our faith. Jesus predicted this: "When you have turned again, strengthen your brothers" (Luke 22:32). A denier of Jesus, strengthening his brothers? How could this be? *Jesus prayed for him.* So the strengthened became the strengthener, the denier became the preacher, the coward became the encourager, and the doubter was filled with faith through the Holy Spirit (Acts 2). Peter turned from his sin, and Jesus used him.

How might God want to use your story to strengthen others? How might he use your weaknesses to build up the church? This is how he works: through weak characters like us whom he strengthens to display the divine drama of his triumph over all evil.

For true followers of Jesus, our turning away from evil's advances isn't an *if;* it's a *when.* Our faith will not fail, because Jesus will not fail us. His work on the cross and his resurrection secure us, and now nothing can separate us from his love—not even sin, failure, or doubt. Even Peter, who messed up badly, was restored—not because he was great, but because Jesus is. Charles Spurgeon once said,

> Remember, therefore, it is not *your hold* of Christ that saves you—it is Christ; it is not *your joy* in Christ that saves you—it is Christ; it is not even faith in Christ, although that is the instrument—it is Christ's blood and merits. Therefore, do not look so much to your hand with which you are grasping Christ as to Christ. . . . Do not look to your faith, but to Jesus, the founder and perfecter of your faith.[4]

Look to Jesus. Listen carefully to him. He is faithfully praying for you, as if he were sitting in the very next room.

Meeting with Jesus

1. Read Ephesians 6:11–12. What difference would it make to your walk with Jesus to take the divine drama seriously? How might it change the way you pray?
2. How would you describe what Jesus is doing right now in heaven? Why is this important to know and believe, especially as you face spiritual struggles and doubts?
3. Consider a time when your faith seemed to fail but the situation served to strengthen your faith and that of others. How does this testify to the power of Jesus's prayers? Journal your answers from above or any remaining questions you have.

20

When Your Faith Flounders

Matthew 11:2–6

Let's take off the spiritual masks we wear for a moment. You know the ones. The mask that says we're okay when we're really not. The mask that says, "God is so good," when deep down we're harboring disappointment or resentment toward him because of an unwanted circumstance. The mask that causes us to raise our voices in song on Sunday morning although we're unwilling to open up the Bible ourselves Monday through Saturday.

Whether we admit it or not, we're all tempted to wear masks—most often because we're ashamed and afraid to admit to ourselves and to others that doubts really do exist.

But I'm going to let you in on a little secret: Every follower of Jesus faces doubts to one degree or another. None of us are immune. Not the pastor, Christian writer, evangelist, overseas missionary, Sunday school teacher, and, no, not even John the Baptist—the very one called to lead the way for the earthly ministry of Jesus.

I'm thankful God included his story in Matthew, because I believe it's both a comfort and a guidepost for us when our own doubts come.

STRONG IN THE SPIRIT, WEAK IN THE FLESH

John the Baptist was a prophet with a unique call on his life. Centuries earlier, Isaiah had prophesied that one would "prepare the way of the Lord in the wilderness [and] make a straight highway for our God in the desert" (Isaiah 40:3, CSB). The prophecy was pointing forward to John the Baptist, who was called by God to prepare the hearts of the people for the arrival of Jesus. Matthew 3 makes it sound like John the Baptist would have been a shoo-in for the show *Survivor.* He'd been living in the wilderness, eating locusts and honey, and clothing himself with camel hair. At age thirty, he began his ministry by calling people to repentance and baptism, declaring, "I baptize you with water for repentance, but he who is coming after me is mightier than I, whose sandals I am not worthy to carry. He will baptize you with the Holy Spirit and fire" (verse 11).

But his calling to prepare hearts for the Messiah's arrival was relatively short-lived. After John (feeling unworthy) reluctantly baptized Jesus, "behold, the heavens were opened to [Jesus], and he saw the Spirit of God descending like a dove and coming to rest on him; and behold, a voice from heaven said, 'This is my beloved Son, with whom I am well pleased'" (verses 16–17). And with that undeniable revelation, the earthly ministry of Jesus had begun.

Can you imagine being in John's sandals? If anyone ever had concrete evidence that Jesus is who he says he is, it was John the Baptist.

But guess what? He still wasn't sure.

Not long after the spiritual high of baptizing the Son of God, John found himself in prison at the hands of Herod Antipas for calling out his unlawful marriage to Herodias. As he sat there, chained in a damp, dark prison, he had an endless amount of time to sit with his thoughts. That's the scene that we come to in Matthew 11:2–3: "When John heard in prison about the deeds of the Christ, he sent word by his disciples and said to him, 'Are you the one who is to come, or shall we look for another?' "

Do you realize what his question implies? John's entire life had been dedicated to testifying to the coming of Jesus. He had just heard the voice of God bear evidence to Jesus's divine identity. Regardless, as he sat in the eerie silence and darkness of prison, whispers of doubt begin to reverberate. *After all I've sacrificed, is Jesus really the Messiah? Was I just a fool, giving everything for nothing?* (Jesus had performed miracles for others. Why wasn't he doing a miracle for John?) This wasn't where John saw his story heading, and it left him vulnerable to doubts and taunts from the enemy.

But here's what we can't miss: John took his concerns directly to Jesus. He didn't allow his questions to fester and turn into bitterness. He sent a message to his friend, seeking reassurance.

And Jesus did just that—with patience, not offense or harshness. He simply offered John the assurance his heart needed: "Go and tell John what you hear and see: the blind receive their sight and the lame walk, lepers are cleansed and the deaf hear, and the dead are raised up, and the poor have good news preached to them. And blessed is the one who is not offended by me" (verses 4–6).

It's as if he were saying, *Yes, John, even though you can't see it with your own eyes right now, I am the one. If you're struggling to take my word for it, here is undeniable evidence.*

But Jesus didn't stop there. He turned to those around him and *boasted* about John, declaring, "Truly, I say to you, among those born of women there has arisen no one greater than John the Baptist" (verse 11). It's striking that Jesus counted John among the greatest to be born immediately after John had expressed his doubts to him. In contrast, all throughout the Gospels, Jesus came down harshly on the self-righteousness and spiritual arrogance of the religious leaders. The former approached Jesus as the source and sustainer of his faith, while the others saw him as a threat to their own perceived goodness.

TAKING DOUBT TO THE SOURCE

Although Jesus does show profound compassion toward our doubts, there are two dangers that we need to be aware of.

The first is living with a hidden shame and guilt because we assume "good Christians" don't question. We fear that if we acknowledge doubts exist, others will condemn us. Or worse, God will.

The second danger is dwelling on our doubts, rehearsing them over and over in our minds. As we do so, they begin to etch a path in our thought life that's difficult to get off.

Over time, doubts undealt with can become the lens through which we view everything, reinforcing those false beliefs every time circumstances seem to confirm our suspicions. If left unchecked, those doubts lead to unbelief. Because of that, the enemy works hard to keep us isolated and silent in the shame of doubt. He convinces us that acknowledging them is of far greater risk than pretending they don't exist.

But there's a better way, and John the Baptist led by example. Not only do we acknowledge the existence of doubts when they come; we also take them directly to the source—God himself. We're deceiving ourselves to think we can somehow hide them from the Lord. Deep down, we know it's ridiculous to believe we can outsmart the God of the universe.

However, there's actually comfort in this unsettling reality. If God knows the past, present, and future, not only does he bear with our doubts today, he also died for us, knowing these doubts would come. "While we were still weak, at the right time Christ died for the ungodly" (Romans 5:6). He gave himself for us, knowing our faith would be weak at times, filled with the cracks of faithless feelings and questions. He understands our limited ability to see all he's doing for our eternal joy. Why, then, do we think he'll reject us for wrestling with our faith?

Friend, harboring hurt, anger, and questions is like letting an infection fester. But taking them to the One who made us and knows us better than ourselves is like taking them to the doctor. As the all-knowing source of lifesaving treatments, he alone has the cure.

Taking our doubts to the Lord is actually a *sign* of faith, not a lack of it. It's saying, "Lord, I'm struggling to believe what you say is true, but I trust you enough to bring all of me (even these questions and unsettling feelings). I'm asking you to heal what is hurting, give wisdom where it's lacking, and give assurance where my faith feels weak." That, my friend, isn't a sign of a spiritually immature Christian. It's a sign of a growing disciple who acknowledges their limited understanding and weakness.

Don't let the fear of others, the pride within, or the lies of the enemy convince you to try to hide the true state of your heart from Jesus. Like he did for John the Baptist, he longs to assure you that he is for you.

TAKING DOUBTS CAPTIVE

I grew up an athlete, loving every sport I came into contact with. As I previously shared, one of the main sports was basketball, and my eyes were set on playing at a Division 1 college. However, during my last year of high school, my world fell apart at the hands of an abusive coach and a devastating injury.

At the time, the painful treatment I endured and the loss of my identity as an athlete sent me spiraling. The God I thought I knew felt cold, cruel, and distant. I didn't know who I was anymore, and I didn't understand why a good God would allow a young girl to be so mistreated and her dreams crushed. Eventually, my spiraling led me to the pediatric psych ward after I hit rock bottom and attempted to take my life.

But it was at rock bottom that I was forced to face my doubts. As painful as it was, God used those days to lead me to wrestle with false beliefs and ask him to show me who he really was, rather than my curated, comfortable version of him.

In God's kindness, sometimes he gives us glimpses of his redeeming purposes through our pain, while many things remain a mystery. I still grieve the loss of being able to do so much of what I love because of my degenerative ankle. God hasn't offered me an explanation wrapped up with a nice little bow. Over the years, I've learned it's okay to be honest about my disappointments, especially when it's hard to see any earthly good that could come from them. If I'm not honest, resentment takes root. But as I've come in humble honesty with my feelings, God has been faithful to lead me to a place of acceptance within the disappointment, helping me trust his loving purposes even when I can't understand them.

We will only further fuel our doubts if we let our thoughts and feelings fester without bringing them honestly to Jesus. Simply telling yourself not to feel a certain way rarely makes a lasting difference. But our minds and hearts *can* be transformed when we bring those thoughts and feelings to the One who has the power to exchange them for a faith and assurance that only he can give through the truth of his Word.

I encourage you to be honest with yourself. What doubts have you wrestled with? And what wrong beliefs have those doubts fostered? Now be honest with the Lord about them. John the Baptist's story encourages us that Jesus won't reject a humble heart that's struggling to believe.

As the prophet Jeremiah declared after years of doubt, sorrow, and suffering because of God's perceived abandonment,

> "[The LORD] will watch over him as a shepherd guards
> his flock,
> for the LORD has ransomed Jacob
> and redeemed him from the power of one stronger than he."

> They will come and shout for joy on the heights of Zion;
> they will be radiant with joy
> because of the LORD's goodness. . . .
> I [the LORD] will turn their mourning into joy,
> give them consolation,
> and bring happiness out of grief. . . .
> My people will be satisfied with my goodness.
> (Jeremiah 31:10-14, CSB)

God *can't* be unfaithful to you, no matter how things may appear. So ask him to show you what's true behind the clouds of doubt and to help you surrender whatever earthly desire you have equated with his goodness. Because Jesus endured this world, he knows how heartbreaking and confusing it can be. He knows that faith without sight is simply *not* natural to our finite minds. But he wants so much more for us than the temporary blessings and ease of this world. He wants to give us peace and assurance beyond what this world can give—and an eternity where faith is finally made sight.

In fact, the very doubts that you fear might cause your faith to fail may be what will drive you to Jesus's love, goodness, and faithfulness like never before.

His thoughts may not be our thoughts, and his ways may not be our ways (Isaiah 55:8), but we can be assured of this—his heart is *always* for us.

Meeting with Jesus

1. Do you think it's okay to doubt and have questions about faith? If not, why do you believe that?
2. What denied hopes and desires (at least from your perspective) tend to stir up the most intense negative emotions in you? Once you pinpoint those specific areas, ask yourself, *How do those feelings relate to the way I see God's goodness and care (or lack of them)?*
3. What doubts have you wrestled with? And what have those doubts caused you to believe or not believe about God? Will you take those to the Lord in honesty today? Consider the questions above and journal your answers if you're able to.

21

When You Feel Alone in Your Doubts

John 20:26–29

Eleven bewildered men stood on a mountain in the presence of the resurrected Christ. These were the disciples he had spent most of his time with, the ones who had watched him defy gravity and tread waves, make wine from water, reverse disease with a touch, and wake dead people as if from sleep. They had known repentance and tasted his forgiveness. They had watched him absorb human hatred, suffer divine wrath, and succumb to the grave.

Now Jesus stood before them, risen in the flesh. You would think that everything now made sense to them, like a thousand-piece puzzle that had *finally* come together. But not exactly. "When they saw him they worshiped him, but some doubted" (Matthew 28:17).

But some doubted. That's honest and a bit unnerving. How could they see the risen Christ and *still* doubt?

FOR THE DOUBTING HEART

If I could see God, I would never doubt him. How many of us have had this thought? *If God would send a sign, change my situation, give a timely word, I would truly believe. All my doubts would be dispelled, and*

I would trust him. But Matthew's gospel disproves our theory. All four gospels do.

As for the subject of human doubt—those scary and stubbornly intrusive thoughts we wish would just go away—the Gospels face it head-on. God's Word doesn't sugarcoat reality, even the hard, harrowing, or embarrassing parts of what it means to be human.

What is Jesus's desire for the doubting heart?

The gospel writers don't leave us guessing, and what a gift this is for us. Friend, if doubts have disturbed your soul, assailed your mind, and caused you to feel like a bad Christian, let the testimony of God's Word comfort you today. He cares about your doubts and has left you with a healing and strengthening balm. Not only the fourfold gospel narratives but also the whole of Scripture attest that he is trustworthy.

We've looked at Matthew, so now let's look at the other three accounts.

MARK: "THEY WERE AFRAID"

The end of Mark's gospel features three women who arrived at Jesus's tomb to anoint him, but they didn't find his body. Instead, they found a young man in a white robe. He told them not to be alarmed, to behold the empty tomb, and to expect an encounter with Jesus.

Their response? "They went out and fled from the tomb, for trembling and astonishment had seized them, and they said nothing to anyone, for they were afraid" (16:8). Mary and the other women were instructed by the young man to tell the other disciples, but fear and doubt sealed their mouths shut.

What kind of writer ends his resurrection story with scared women? The honest kind. *Astonishment. Fear. Silence.* Mark is describing us.

LUKE: "AN IDLE TALE"

As for Luke's account, he doesn't mince words. He starts with the women's perplexed minds and fear-laden hearts at the tomb (24:1–5) and follows with the disciples' raised eyebrows at their "idle tale" (verses 10–11). He continues with the foolishness of two men who talked with Jesus but had no idea who he was (verses 13–35) and ends with Jesus appearing in Jerusalem (verses 36–43).

Jesus's disciples looked on, frightened and convinced they were seeing a ghost. "Why are you troubled, and why do doubts arise in your hearts?" Jesus asked them (verse 38).

He could ask us the same question.

JOHN: "UNLESS I SEE"

No one was quite as reluctant as Thomas. Poor doubting Thomas! If he had only known how his story would go down in church history. Yet this is perhaps the one we most need to hear.

For some unknown reason, Thomas was absent when Jesus first appeared, and when he heard about it, he was incredulous: "Unless I see in his hands the mark of the nails, and place my finger into the mark of the nails, and place my hand into his side, I will never believe" (John 20:25).

Jesus rebuked him, refused to show himself, and Thomas was lost.

No, that's not Thomas's story, and thank God. Though Thomas's heart was standoffish and guarded, Jesus still drew near. He brought compassion, not condemnation.

> "Peace be with you." Then he said to Thomas, "Put your finger here, and see my hands; and put out your hand, and place it in my side. Do not disbelieve, but believe." Thomas answered him, "My Lord and my God!" Jesus said to him, "Have you believed because you have seen

> me? Blessed are those who have not seen and yet have believed." (verses 26–29)

FAITH'S COMPANION

God is so good to us in his Word. His desire for our doubting hearts is to strengthen our faith by his words of truth and grace. This is why he's given us the whole of Scripture, with its stories that emphasize the humanity of his people—including their confusion, fears, questions, and doubts.

We tend to think faith is the absence of doubt, but doubt usually indicates the presence of faith. Doubt is possible only when there is something to doubt.

Friend, doubt is not the enemy of faith but faith's companion. It's an invitation to know and trust our Savior more. In the church, it's unhealthy to keep our doubts hush-hush—to hide them behind a facade of faith. We need to admit our questions, confront our disbelief, and bathe everything in the clarifying witness of Jesus's Word.

He's given us the truth for good reasons. One of them is dealing with our inevitable doubts. After all, we live by faith in a God we can't see. This is the essence of faith. And if we can't bring our weak faith and wandering thoughts to one another and to the Lord, where can we turn? Certainly not to anything good or helpful, which is why so many have made a shipwreck of their faith, deconstructing until doubt has won the day.

The Gospels prove that, even in the midst of doubt, we can still pursue Jesus. That's why God gave these narratives to us—because we, too, are human, and Jesus, the God-man, knows what we need.

WHAT TO DO WITH YOUR DOUBTS

So what about that thought, *If I could see God, I would never doubt him*? Thomas did see him, and Jesus said, "Blessed are those who have not seen and yet have believed" (John 20:29). He was talking about you and me. This statement is for us, whose eyes haven't seen the risen body of Jesus but whose hearts behold him by faith.

Jesus says to us, "You have not seen me, but you will be blessed as you trust me anyway." What does this look like? How can we cultivate a stronger faith even as we struggle with doubt? How do we pursue the blessing that comes from believing?

Search the Scriptures

When questions come, the world will tell us to journey to different lands, when in fact the treasures of faith are buried right beneath our feet. We just need to dig and seek in order to find. Peter knew this. When all the other disciples left Jesus because his teaching was hard to hear, Jesus asked his remaining friends, "Do you want to go away as well?" Like Peter's, our faith grows when we answer as he did, "Lord, to whom shall we go? You have the words of eternal life" (John 6:67–68).

Take your questions and complaints straight to God in his Word. Let the light and truth of Scripture stream into the murky fog of your doubts. This may not happen quickly or in the way you expect. But it is better to walk by faith as you wait on the Lord than to walk by sight and forsake his blessing. Make the prayer of the psalmist your own as you search the Scriptures, and know that this endeavor is entirely worth your every effort:

> You are my hiding place and my shield;
>   I hope in your word. . . .
> Uphold me according to your promise, that I may live,
>   and let me not be put to shame in my hope!
>   (Psalm 119:114, 116)

Seek the Spirit

Yet our own effort isn't enough. If we open God's Word in our own strength, with our own insight, we won't get very far. However, with God's help and strength, his Word will accomplish his work within us—however slowly—and that work is powerful and effective. "The Spirit of God works in, with, and through, the Word of God," Colin Smith says. "And in the Word and the Spirit we have a double defense against the power of lies and deception."[1] So, as you search the Scriptures, seek the Holy Spirit.

Many times, I'm quick to approach reading God's words in my own strength and understanding, checking off boxes and "doing it right," but it will all fall flat without his help. After all, it was the Spirit who breathed out God's words in the first place (Ephesians 6:17; 2 Timothy 3:16). Ask God to give you eyes to see his light, ears to hear his truth, and a heart to trust his ways—especially when doubts come. Open his Word and pray, "God, I *want* to believe. Help my unbelief. Open my eyes, Holy Spirit, so I will see your truth and walk in it." He will be faithful to answer, even over time and in unexpected ways.

Suspect Your Doubts

Often the problems that arise from doubt outweigh those that arise from faith. Try tracing your doubts all the way to their necessary end. For example, if you're questioning the existence of God, then try to imagine how *your* existence would make any sense without his: *If there is no benevolent, almighty Creator and we are nothing more than cells, then where do we get our urge for purpose, our hunger for love, and our ache for glory?* Ask yourself what it would be like to live a hopeless and meaningless existence and if you truly believe that's our reality. If you're questioning the validity of the Bible and you wonder if it's all just a bunch of random words from random people, then ask, *How is the storyline so cohesive, and why did Jesus himself seem to trust it?*

Our doubts present many more difficulties than we may first believe, but we have to be willing to go there. When we're tempted to suspect God's truth, we also need to suspect our doubts.

Learn from the Past

We tend to think that our cultural moment is the most advanced and impressive one, but we are one blip in history, and there is much to learn from the past. When I was walking through a hard season of physical pain (and the doubts that arose with it), Susannah Spurgeon's story encouraged my weary heart.[2] Apologetics, biography, and church history will help us solidify what we believe. While we want God's Word to be our primary source, we can also benefit from theologians, historians, and suffering saints who faced their doubts and grew stronger in trusting God. Let God's faithfulness in the past bolster you in the present.[3]

Pray with Others

Remember, you are not alone in your questioning and fears. The church of Jesus is with you. (The early church too—clearly!) When my faith has felt weak, especially in painful seasons, I've needed to stuff my pride and confess my wandering thoughts to my church family, asking for their help in prayer.

Burying our doubts produces weeds of unbelief, but unearthing them brings them into the piercing light of God's truth and his people—the very people he has provided to strengthen our faith in Jesus (Ephesians 4:11–16). We also have the opportunity to "have mercy on those who doubt" (Jude 22), just as Jesus has been merciful to us and all those before us—Thomas included.

"Blessed are those who have not seen and yet have believed" (John 20:29).

WORSHIP IN YOUR DOUBTS

Aren't you thankful for Jesus's words to his struggling friend? Isn't it relieving to know that the Bible addresses the very thing we're so tempted to hide? Worship and doubt aren't mutually exclusive; the two can (and often do) exist together. We pursue by faith what we can't see, so when Christ appears—scars and all—we will know, without question, that it was all true. *He* was true.

Meeting with Jesus

1. How do the gospel accounts, filled with doubting disciples, encourage you to face your doubts and worship Jesus through them?
2. Respond to the statement "Doubt is faith's companion." Do you agree? Why or why not?
3. Which of these next steps do you want to pursue, even this week (search the Scriptures, seek the Spirit, suspect your doubts, learn from the past, pray with others)? What might that look like?

PART 6

GRIEF

22

When Death Seems to Win

John 11:35

What causes God to weep?

It's a strange thought, God weeping. We don't often think of him that way. It feels too weak, too messy, too . . . human. But if we don't have a category for God weeping, the Bible certainly does. It expands our small, anemic view of who God is, unboxing him and letting him be who he says he is—someone who grieves. In Scripture, God reveals himself as one with a robust emotional life, and boy, do we need this truth.[1] When grief crashes down on us, like waves bowling over a child at the beach, we need someone who understands. We need someone to enter the water alongside us, to hold us above the waves when we're going under. We need someone to drag us onto shore, to sit beside us as we catch our breath. To remain with us in our grief.

We need a God who knows what it is to weep.

JESUS WEPT

One of the shortest verses in the Bible might also be the most profound: "Jesus wept" (John 11:35). Just two words, and our whole perspective shifts. The Creator of heaven and earth isn't some far-off deity; he's a relational God who became human and broke down in tears.[2] The Upholder of the universe let down his emotional guard.

What led to this tearful display, this unfiltered weeping that moves us so?

The death of a friend. As we've seen, Lazarus died after Jesus had delayed his visit. He was sick; now he was gone. One breath, and total expiration. Death had won, and the grave now held its prize. After four long, agonizing days, Jesus arrived at Bethany. He entered death's dominion, its heavy shroud threatening to stifle all hope. And as he looked around, seeing Mary's and Martha's tear-streaked faces, hearing the wailing of mourners, he saw everything that was wrong with everything. He saw the curse of sin. He saw death winning.

Death. It's your greatest enemy, and mine. It isn't something you can control or coerce. It won't listen to you or abide by your plans. It isn't deterred by your clever, lighthearted attempts to ignore it or your strong-willed attempts to evade it. Death reigns, and it is no one's servant (Romans 5:14, 17). No human avoids it, and every living being succumbs to it. You are dust, and to dust you shall return—not by choice, but by death's indiscriminating power (Ecclesiastes 3:19–20).

In the face of such a ruinous enemy and as grief surrounded him on every side, Jesus wept. The limbic system within his brain signaled emotional sadness, and his lacrimal glands responded. The tears fell as God incarnate cried. And we so badly need to see him weep.

DEATH'S TOUCH

As we enter the final stretch of this book, a section on grief, we wonder how it will apply to us. Maybe you don't need to guess, because death has been a too-close reality and you know the force of its waves. You know its heavy shroud, its vice grip, the crushing inability to breathe in its presence. You know what it's like to weep in death's face. Or maybe this doesn't exactly describe you, and yet you know the world has gone terribly sad. Human grief doesn't apply only to death; it applies to everything death has touched:

> Our weakness, our daily advance toward the dust.
> Our fear and shame, the suffocating effects of sin.
> Our loneliness, the souring of relationship.
> Our pain, the betrayal of our earthly bodies.
> Our doubt, the testing of our faith through all the above.

So we grieve. Not in all the same ways, but ultimately over the same enemy.

In the past two weeks, death has come knocking. I've never thought so much about the brevity of human life. One cancer diagnosis, two, then three. National tragedies resulting from broken minds and flash floods. A reading of Ecclesiastes and a reminder of vanity. Ongoing chronic pain alerting me to frailty. Immortal souls rejecting their only hope of eternal joy. Death's touch—or, rather, its terror—is everywhere, and it leaves me scrambling for a foothold, a refuge. Where do we turn when the darkness of death seems to be winning, when fear abounds, when the grief feels like too much to bear?

We look at the man weeping hot tears in front of a tomb.

WHEN GOD WEEPS

What causes Jesus to weep? It's a question worth asking. If God, the perfect and holy One, is grieving, it means we should too. It means we have permission to feel. We're made in his image, and while our emotions are imperfect and untrustworthy at times, they're meant to mirror God's. In a culture that apologizes for tears and ignores death, we need God to tell us what real grief looks like. We need to know what makes God weep. What made Jesus break down in tears that awful day in Bethany?

First, Jesus wept over the agonizing burden of suffering. Have you noticed the contagious nature of tears? When you're surrounded by sadness and the room is heavy with grief or when you're looking into the bleary eyes of a friend as they break down before you, it's hard not to cry. "It is human nature," Ryle says, "that grief is contagious."[3] Suffering carries a burden of tears. What was the cause of Jesus weeping before his friend's tomb? All the crying going on around him. "Jesus saw [Mary] weeping, and the Jews who had come with her also weeping" (John 11:33). When sadness is palpable, grief is communal. So Jesus wept. And when you weep, he cries alongside you.

The book of Hebrews says that Jesus is "touched with the feeling of our infirmities" (4:15, KJV). We often say that something touched our hearts. Jesus's heart is touched by all that touches us. His compassion is drawn out to us, so much that he feels what we feel. This means he knows exactly where and how to meet you today, in whatever grief you are experiencing. If the Son of God displayed such sympathy while he walked on earth, weeping with Mary and Martha, how much more now that he is in heaven will he weep with you?[4] This is Hebrews's point. Jesus knows the breadth and depth of your sorrow, and he will meet you there.

What about our confusion? Sometimes there's no knowing what in the world God is doing when pain and trials come. Mary and Martha both felt this when they said, "Lord, if you had been here, my brother would not have died" (John 11:21, 32). Even the Jews questioned him: "Could not he who opened the eyes of the blind man also have kept this man from dying?" (verse 37). Hard questions haunt us. We are not alone in wondering, *God, where are you?*

Why did you not stop the degenerative cells, the drunk driver, the hurricane, the miscarriage? Suffering can feel like a heavy door shut in our faces, with God on the other side.[5]

These questions would take an entire book to explore, and we won't pretend to answer them here. For now, we receive the Bible's invitation to bring all our hard questions and confusion to Jesus. He won't turn you away for doing so. Actually, questioning his doings affirms his goodness. If God weren't good, we would have no reason to complain or be troubled. But we do and we are, because we want to believe God is good. So we lament.

Maybe the most incredible part of this story is how Jesus wept on the brink of rejoicing. He knew his Father's will—that he would raise Lazarus from the grave. That was always the plan. So why didn't that overshadow the grief? Why didn't it turn away the tears? Because a true human can't help but feel all that's wrong with this world—especially when that human has an eternal soul made for another land. Jesus did, and he gives us permission to do the same.

Before we rush to resurrection, we sit in the solemnity of death.

In times of deep anguish, trite answers and platitudes won't do. Even the powerful truths of our everlasting hope, when misapplied, can feel like salt in a gaping wound.[6] Jesus wept. Do we? Have we found freedom to lament and grieve, and do we bring others such freedom when they suffer? Friend, look at your Savior. He sank to the ground in front of the grave, or perhaps he wet his friends' shoulders with his crying, but there he was, weeping, taking the time to feel suffering's agonizing burden, to mourn what death had touched. It is only right that we do too. If we don't, we miss the chance to know the Savior who weeps with us, who draws near in our mourning. We miss the heart of him who cries with us in our pain.

And we miss his rage over death, the cause of it all.

Second, Jesus wept over the repulsive nature of death. Where do we turn when the darkness of death seems to be winning, when the grief feels like too much to bear? We look at the man full of indignation at evil. "When Jesus saw [Mary] weeping, and the Jews who had come with her also weeping, *he was deeply moved in his spirit* and greatly troubled" (John 11:33). Before Jesus wept, he got angry—really angry. The phrase "deeply moved" comes from a Greek word used to describe a snorting horse.[7] "So we find Jesus," Eric Schumacher says, "staring death in the face, full of indignation, snorting in anger at his enemy."[8] Jesus felt holy agitation toward death and all sin's other devastating effects. He hates everything death has wrought, and he hates what it's done to you.

When you feel overcome by death's touch and overpowered by its presence, see Jesus raging at death. Sometimes we want to get past our angry emotions, and if we aren't ready for that, other people want us to move on. But death leaves an indelible mark. The only shot we have at moving toward a hope of glory starts with acknowledging what will make it so glorious—the complete eradication of death. And that requires *feeling* how repulsive death is. When everything within us rages against it, we testify that there's a heaven. We shout that everything is not okay. We hearken back to a time when it once was, before death ruined it all, when peace reigned, our souls aching in "memory of the world unbroken."[9]

So, yes, we are angry, and that's as it should be. But we can't let our anger at death consume us, because that would mean death has won. Instead, we look at the man lying prostrate in the garden, sweating drops of blood. We look instead at what he has done to death.

WHEN DEATH DIES

There was once a garden in which everything was wonderful, but by one man's selfish choice, death cursed all. So death reigned. Then there was another garden in which everything was terrible, but by another man's selfless choice, death would be disarmed. The first man prayed, "Not your will, Father, but mine be done," and ruined everything. The second man prayed, "Not my will, Father, but yours be done," and would redeem it all.

"With loud cries and tears" (Hebrews 5:7), his body so overwhelmed with sorrow that his sweat glands produced blood instead, Jesus wept and raged at death—its fatal touch, its fatal cost—and faced it head-on at Calvary, where it would receive its fatal blow.

Jesus became the curse of death and at the same time dissolved Adam's curse.[10]

And one day he will destroy this last enemy once and for all (1 Corinthians 15:26).

Friend, this is your hope when death leaves its indelible mark and seems to be winning: the nail-scarred hands of one who knows it, hates it, and weeps for it—and who has done something about it.

Meeting with Jesus

1. What kind(s) of grief are you currently experiencing? In your own words, how would you describe what makes death's touch so hard? Write out Psalm 56:8–9 and make it your prayer.
2. In what ways does it help you to envision Jesus weeping before Lazarus's tomb? How does this translate to his presence in heaven and his ability to know what you're feeling?
3. "When everything within us rages against death, we testify that there's a heaven." Do you agree? Why or why not? How does Jesus's rage toward and conquering of death fuel our hope?

23

When Grief Dulls Your Senses

Mark 14:34

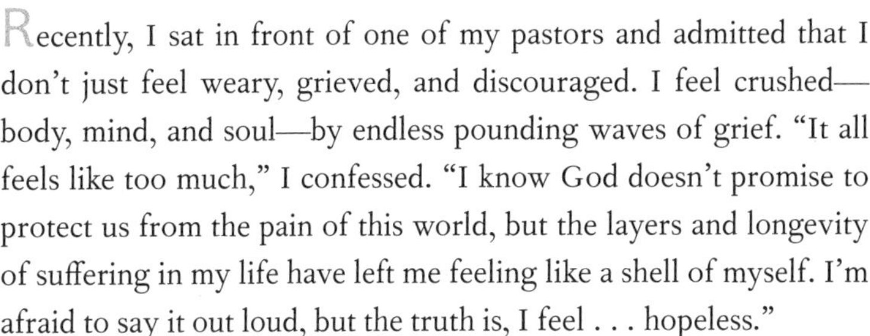

Recently, I sat in front of one of my pastors and admitted that I don't just feel weary, grieved, and discouraged. I feel crushed—body, mind, and soul—by endless pounding waves of grief. "It all feels like too much," I confessed. "I know God doesn't promise to protect us from the pain of this world, but the layers and longevity of suffering in my life have left me feeling like a shell of myself. I'm afraid to say it out loud, but the truth is, I feel . . . hopeless."

Some seasons are like that. They aren't just overwhelming. They aren't just hard. They're paralyzing, and from a human standpoint—they feel unbearable.

In these seasons, life turns into a blur. Food loses its taste, community sounds exhausting, what you used to enjoy becomes dull, decisions feel impossible, and tears become the only language you know how to speak. Sometimes grief feels beyond what we can endure.

It sounds similar to Jesus's words in Gethsemane: " 'My soul is very sorrowful, even to death' " (Mark 14:34) and "Being in agony he prayed more earnestly; and his sweat became like great drops of blood falling down to the ground" (Luke 22:44).

Jesus is no stranger to unimaginable sorrow. As he carried the weight of the world on his shoulders, he was physically and emotionally crushed to the point of sweating drops of blood.

And yet, despite feeling crushed by grief and sorrow, he lifted his head, cried out to his Father, and stepped toward the cross. In Jesus's humanity, it was impossible, but with his Father's strength, he endured it.

Friend, if you're enduring a season that feels unbearable right now, know this: Jesus sees how hard it is to get up in the morning. He understands when you feel overwhelmed by the smallest of tasks. And as one who has endured the greatest level of grief imaginable, he is patient and compassionate toward you. He sees the heavy weight of your affliction—including every tear you have shed. Joni Eareckson Tada reminds us,

> He is moved by your tears. Remember, He places your tears in His bottle (Ps. 56:8 KJV). Now there's a reason God's Word describes it that way—because in a bottle, our tears won't evaporate. They won't disappear. God's compassion is so great that He remembers your afflictions for all time.
>
> What's more, in a bottle He can *weigh* your tears. Those tears represent how *long* you've suffered.[1]

God cares *so* much—not just about the other side of the suffering, but about the disorienting, painful middle—that he holds, remembers, and cares about the cost of your tears.

Most importantly, Jesus promises to meet you with the strength you need to take the next step, even when sorrow and tears leave you sucked dry of strength.

DO THE NEXT THING

So how do we survive when everything in us wants to escape but we can't? How do we practically live when our minds and bodies feel paralyzed by the weight of grief? How do we press on when pain dulls our senses?

As Elisabeth Elliot (wife of martyred missionary Jim Elliot) often quoted from a poem, "Do the next thing."[2]

Do the next thing that has to be done. Roll your unwilling body out of bed. Get the kids to school. Run the one errand that can't be put off another day. Read or listen to the next chapter in your Bible reading plan. Do one task that's most needed today. Make that one important phone call at work.

Then throw the frozen pizza in the oven and throw the shame that comes with it right in the trash.

Because life is lived just one moment at a time. And when it feels too crushing to look two steps ahead, simply take the step that's right in front of you. After you do, trust that God will give you the strength to take the next step when it comes.

At times, it's wise to simplify life and take it in bite-sized chunks, recognizing that our humanity has its limitations, especially when weighed down by this world. But how?

Here are a few practical suggestions.

Call One Friend or Mentor

Find one or two trusted friends or mentors and invite them to bear your sorrows with you. The enemy will try to convince you that no one wants to hear it, nobody can handle it, and you're just a burden. But even Jesus, the Son of God, knew he needed the prayers and support of his disciples as he bore the weight of sorrow and grief (as imperfect as their efforts may have been). God calls other believers to bear our burdens with us (Galatians 6:2), so be willing to take the risk and allow a trusted friend or mentor to enter into your sorrow—even if they do so imperfectly.

It may be messy. But messy is where the gospel meets real life.

Meditate on One Scripture

You may not feel capable of digesting large chunks of Scripture in this season, but don't neglect God's Word because your capacity is limited. Open the Bible one more time. Write down one more verse that speaks encouragement and hope, and after you do, do it again one more time tomorrow. Instead of your grief driving you away from the Lord, allow it to drive you nearer to him as the only One who can fully understand and bear it with you.

Jesus could do nothing but cry out in desperation to his Father as grief literally poured out of his body. Worship right now may simply look like resting in one or two truths that assure your weary heart that God is for you and will be faithful to his promises.

Reflect on One Good Gift

As difficult as it may seem, attempt to acknowledge one thing you have to be grateful for, one thing of beauty around you, or one way you see God faithfully providing for you amid the hard. It may take a minute to find it, but strain the eyes of your heart to look through the lens of gratitude and beauty, and remind yourself of the gift it is.

As Jesus looked toward the cross, his grief accurately reflected the horrific reality of what he was about to endure, but he walked through it "for the joy that was set before him" (Hebrews 12:2). And that joy was rooted in his profound love for you and me.

Therefore, even if it feels impossible to muster earthly gratitude in your acute distress, you can still have deep assurance that what feels crushing right now doesn't have the power to overcome you. Jesus was crushed—body, mind, and soul—on our behalf to break that power over us. As we taste the bitterness of death in our earthly grief, we are drawn into a deeper understanding of the ultimate depths that Jesus's human and divine anguish plumbed for us. His sacrifice now assures us that grief won't have the final word.

God doesn't ask us to be grateful *for* our circumstances, but he wants us to remember what we still have to be grateful for *in* our circumstances. We may not be able to choose what's happening around us, but we can choose the lens we view it all through.

I encourage you today, even if life feels absolutely crushing, to ask God to help you cling to the hope of the gospel. Ask him to help you see the very real and present help of Jesus and see one way he's providing for you in this seemingly impossible season.

Rehearse One Act of God's Faithfulness

There's a reason God repeatedly told his people to "remember" in the Bible. We are a very forgetful people. Because of that, God knew we would need to frequently remind ourselves of his past faithfulness—especially when he seems silent to our cries for help.

The writers of the Gospels often recall Old Testament prophecies and promises that prove God's faithfulness to fulfill every single one of them. Today, look back and recall when you saw God's faithfulness to you, despite not seeing any way forward at the time. Consider a time when he didn't provide the answer you desired but instead met you in a way that drew you closer to him, to experience his strength and presence like never before.

My weary friend, choose to rehearse God's past faithfulness today, even when everything seems hopeless and unbearable.

Allow Yourself One Simple Enjoyment

When our spirit is broken, it's hard to find enjoyment in anything. We struggle to take notice of and enjoy even the small things. This week, what would it look like for you to enjoy something as a good gift from God, even if it doesn't change your circumstances?

Make that extra cup of coffee or tea. Go for a walk and soak in the quiet and fresh air. Sit and watch the sunset. Eat your favorite meal. Watch a clean comedy to remember the gift of laughter. Carve out a little time to enjoy a hobby. Take twenty minutes to read a book or pray. Give yourself permission to smile and enjoy the simple things, even if there doesn't seem to be much to smile about these days.

Because Jesus took our sorrows on himself, we now have the gift of his comfort in our grief, the gift of his strength to take the next step, and the gift of his presence to experience glimpses of joy, as God's tangible love is poured out to us through his Spirit.

Remind Yourself It Won't Last Forever

It feels like grief will last forever, but it won't. These sorrows and the crushing weight of this world won't last forever, because Jesus bore our grief to the point of death. And because he didn't stay there, defeating death by rising again, our grief now has an end date. Until then, it's okay to acknowledge our humanity and limitations. God isn't asking us to know how we'll endure tomorrow or even five steps ahead. He asks us to lean on his strength and grace one moment at a time.

This season may feel crushing to your spirit, but if you are in Christ, you won't be in this place forever. For "the LORD is close to the brokenhearted and saves those who are crushed in spirit" (Psalm 34:18, NIV).

Weary friend, right now you may not feel capable of much. But God doesn't need you to be. We are held, not because we're faithful enough, strong enough, or unbreakable, but because he is. So close your eyes, take a deep breath, and remind yourself that you will not be crushed, because Jesus was crushed on your behalf.

Draw near to his sustaining grace and take the next step in his strength.

Meeting with Jesus

1. What circumstance right now feels overwhelming or crushing? Write out Psalm 34:18 and journal some thoughts about how this applies to your circumstance.
2. How is this circumstance affecting you emotionally, physically, mentally, and spiritually? Be honest with the Lord about your answer out loud or in your journal.
3. Out of the suggestions above, what is one practical and small step you can take today in faith that Jesus will meet you there?

24

When the World Moves On Without You

Matthew 14:10–14

That night—like countless days and nights before it—something triggered my child's neurological illness, and all bets were off. Irrational and uncontrollable rage overtook him, and after hours of a physical and verbal war, I was left exhausted with emotional and physical wounds that told a story only I knew in full. Our child was tormented, our family was suffering the effects, and worst of all, most had no framework for the extreme nature of his illness. In the early months and years of his growing challenges, many friends and family did their best to enter into our heartache to encourage and help as they were able. But as time went on and it became clear that his challenges weren't going anywhere, many grew weary of our lives always being so full of difficulty. Our grief wasn't a slow-healing wound; it was a wound being ripped back open every day. Understandably, that wasn't an easy weight for others to bear along with us for the long haul, so many relationships grew shallow and distant. They were close enough to be friendly but far enough to keep our clouds from blocking their sunlight. Over time, I learned the art of sanitizing my life to protect others from the circumstances and grief that seemed like too much for them to bear.

I remained frozen in grief while the world went on without me.

JESUS HAS BEEN THERE

As we've discussed in depth, the Gospels give us a bird's-eye view of the personal life of Jesus. These accounts show that he truly became as we are—including experiencing grief.

Do you recall the passage in Matthew that details John the Baptist's imprisonment (11:2–6)? Instead of John being let out of prison, his days came to a screeching halt when Herod's wicked wife asked for his head on a platter—and her request was granted. Immediately, John's disciples went to tell Jesus about John's death, and soon after, we see the humanity of Jesus on display: "When Jesus heard this, he withdrew from there in a boat to a desolate place by himself" (14:13).

Understandably, he wanted to be alone. His friend had just been killed. Despite knowing that death and evil were part of this broken world and despite knowing that he had come to defeat both, Jesus grieved the loss of his faithful servant John. Like any of us would, he wanted the space to grieve.

But that's easier said than done when you're Jesus. His world may have just been rocked, but no one else seemed to notice: "When the crowds heard it, they followed him on foot from the towns" (verse 13).

Jesus knows what it's like when people want more from you in the midst of your grief. He knows what it's like to feel a gaping hole in your heart while others expect you to move on. And he has compassion—in ways far greater than we could ever comprehend.

Somehow, even in Jesus's grief, his empathy toward others drove him more than his own pain: "When he went ashore he saw a great crowd, and he had compassion on them and healed their sick" (verse 14). Not only does he know heartache; he is also drawn toward it with God-sized compassion.

Does God feel distant from your suffering right now? Be encouraged—Jesus was so drawn toward the pain of others that it overcame his own grief when he walked this earth. He draws near to you with that same love and compassion today.

JESUS SEES, EVEN WHEN OTHERS DON'T

There's something about profound tragedy and grief that changes us, especially when it involves the loss of someone we love or the life we once knew. We're different from who we were before the world we knew (or expected) unraveled. Death leaves a gaping hole never to be filled in the same way on earth. A painful, life-altering diagnosis changes everything, shaking beliefs that once seemed so easy to believe. And tragedy shatters the rose-colored glasses that once painted the world with such beautiful colors.

But for everyone else untouched by the same reality, life goes on as usual—not because they're heartless, but because your trials haven't changed their immediate world. They still have to-do lists to accomplish, schedules to run, work to be done, and their own worries. Even more, many sufferings go mostly unseen. The wife who's grieving her husband's affair but who's unsure of what's appropriate to share, the husband and wife who feel gutted by a third miscarriage, the chronically ill person who functions at half the capacity they once did, the parent raising a neurodivergent child who most people assume just needs more discipline at home—and the list goes on.

Whether our loss and grief are visible or not, loneliness is always a close companion. Why? Because no one—and I mean no one—can fully enter into those secret places where the human spirit suffers. Even if someone experiences something similar, our temperament, our support system, our past, and countless other realities influence the way we experience grief. Although others may be compassionate and helpful, there's still much they can't understand, because they're not you.

That's why there's such comfort in knowing Jesus sees and intimately knows all of us. We don't have to exhaust ourselves explaining why we feel the way we do or trying to justify the depth of our pain, because he already knows it in full. He knows how years of challenges have multiplied this loss. He knows how your friend's pregnancy announcement made the pain of your miscarriage more palpable, even though you truly want to rejoice with her. And he knows how disability or illness has left you feeling even more isolated, magnifying the silence that swallows your cries.

It's easy to feel like the servant girl Hagar in the Old Testament, who sat rejected and alone in the wilderness. But God saw her when no one else did—and in love he drew near. He is El Roi, the God who sees (Genesis 16:13). And not only does he see you; he also comes running with arms of compassion.

JESUS STAYS, EVEN WHEN OTHERS MOVE ON

I think we can all agree that it's difficult for many to stick around in both acute grief and seasons of long-suffering. If we're honest, we struggle to be that person for another. The fact of the matter is, suffering makes us uncomfortable. Not because we don't care, but because it's difficult to sit in another's pain. We feel helpless to do anything about it. Sometimes we have this unspoken fear that if we get too close to suffering, it might become our reality too. Or sadly, in our selfishness, we'd simply rather not have our comfortable little bubble burst by another's pain. Other times busyness tempts us to believe grieving with others will require too much time and effort.

Even the most thoughtful, compassionate person in the world will never be there for us in a perfect sense. Think of it this way: When someone loses an arm, others can grieve that loss with them, but they won't feel the full loss of the arm when they still have the use of two. That's not indifference or lack of compassion; it's simply the limitations we face as human beings. That's why, in the immediate aftermath of a tragedy or in the initial days of long-suffering, there's a flood of comfort, grieving friends and family, and practical help. But before long, the crowds begin to thin, the meals become infrequent, and loneliness fills their place.

It's easy, of course, to blame others for being uncaring when they begin to move on from our grief. And it's true—some seem to have far less compassion to give than others. But I can assure you, that perspective will lead only to bitterness, self-pity, and, ultimately, greater loneliness. If we're expecting others to be and give what only God can, people will always let us down. Every human being has a limited capacity, unable to be fully invested everywhere without dropping the ball somewhere. Even if everything in a person wishes they could, they simply can't. Only Jesus, who has unlimited capacity and full understanding, can stick by our side in the way we truly long to be cared for. And that's by his design, or we would run to the world rather than to him.

I've often been encouraged by how many times God says to us in the Bible, "I will never leave you or forsake you." He must have known that we would need the constant reminder. Over and over again, God assures those whom he calls his own that he will never leave or forsake them. So today I encourage you to take your eyes off those who you wish would stick around and instead look to the One who's been there all along: "It is the Lord who goes before you. He will be with you; he will not leave you or forsake you. Do not fear or be dismayed" (Deuteronomy 31:8).

JESUS STRENGTHENS, EVEN WHEN OTHERS CAN'T

During one of the hardest seasons with our son's illness, a woman I now consider one of my dearest friends (but barely knew at the time) sent me a note of encouragement in the mail. One of her comments struck me: *"I know there's not much I can do to help, but I just want you to know that the endurance of your faith has challenged and encouraged me in my own faith."* They were genuinely words of comfort. It felt like a glimpse of something redemptive out of such seemingly pointless suffering. But she also acknowledged her limitations, knowing there was only so much she could do.

Some think they have more to offer than they do, and it ends up hurting, while others know they have little to practically offer but still show up with the comfort of their presence. But no one can give us the strength we most need. Only Someone who knows all things (including every iota of our being) and is the very essence of strength can infuse us with the courage and ability to put one foot in front of the other. In Isaiah 41:10, the Lord declared,

> Fear not, for I am with you;
>   be not dismayed, for I am your God;
> I will strengthen you, I will help you,
>   I will uphold you with my righteous right hand.

If you have put your trust in Jesus as Savior and Lord, God is with you, and you have what you need to face the days ahead. He will strengthen you. He will help you. And he will uphold you with the strength of his own presence.

Sometimes it takes our world stopping to see that Jesus has been there all along, ready and willing to meet us with his forgiveness in our sin, his compassion in our pain, his comfort in our loss, and his strength in our weakness.

Let your grief, and the loneliness it has brought, lead you to the endlessly compassionate heart of Jesus. Not only has he experienced the full extent of grief, but he also sees the full earth-shattering effects of yours. Even more, he beckons you to bring all of yourself to him in faith with the promise that he will never leave you or forsake you and will give you the strength you need to endure what lies ahead. Your world may feel like it has stopped. But while the world has moved on, Jesus hasn't.

He's here to stay.

Meeting with Jesus

1. How does this chapter most relate to you? Read Psalm 69:1–3, 13–18 and journal these verses as your own words of lament to the Lord.
2. If you're grieving right now, which of these areas have you struggled with the most? How does knowing that Jesus sees and draws near in your pain bring comfort?
3. If you haven't experienced a season of grief, how have you responded to others in theirs? Ask the Lord to help you draw near to someone in your life who's hurting, even in your limitations.

25

When You Long for Jesus to Make It Right

John 16:1–33

We live in the land in-between. In this beautiful, terrible land of waiting, our fallen frames groan for trouble to be resolved, for wounds to heal. And we are not alone in our groaning, for even the created universe longs to be released from death's touch, to be set free from its corrupting grip (Romans 8:19–22). The grief we feel over our humanity—over our not-enoughness and slow deterioration back to dust—comes in many forms, but grief abounds and burdens us.

In this in-between land, we are not yet home.

A STARTLING ANNOUNCEMENT

We aren't the only ones affected by this discouragement. Peter, James, John, and the rest of the disciples assumed Jesus's kingly rule was right here and right now—that their Messiah would surely save God's people from Roman oppression. They didn't grasp that the messianic prophecies would be fulfilled over time in the slow but sure coming of God's eternal kingdom. So, after many healings and other miracles and after three years of preaching and teaching, the words that came from Jesus's mouth weren't what they expected or wanted to hear: "Little children, yet a little while I am with you. You will seek me, and just as I said to the Jews, so now I also say to you, 'Where I am going you cannot come'" (John 13:33).

Wait—what, Jesus? You're leaving? And we can't follow you to where you're going? Imagine their disbelief. They had been close with their Master, listening to his words and meeting with him for three straight years—but now he was telling them they couldn't any longer. At least not the way they once had.

Jesus was saying goodbye. For now.

This isn't the way it's supposed to be, they likely thought. Peter responded like a little kid to a parent who was about to leave: "Lord, where are you going?" (verse 36). And isn't that how we often feel? *Lord, where are you? Where have you gone? Don't you care about me?* We feel left behind or maybe left to fend for ourselves. Faced with the complexities of being human and the many griefs of this in-between world, we can feel like Jesus is so far away.

In God's kindness, he gives us one particular section of Scripture, John 13–17, to answer some of our questions and comfort our weary, waiting hearts. Ultimately, he does this by telling us about his Spirit.

A PROMISED HELPER

This summer, our family marks five years in our current home, and we love remembering the story of how we found it. God's hand led us to it, in just the right timing, and to our delight the previous owners were Christians. More than that, they were members of our church. And even more, we knew them personally, and my husband had held youth ministry events in their house. Our realtor thought we were crazy when we walked through it and told her, "This is it. No need to look further." But we were sure. This place was ours—it had our names written on its walls—so we placed a down payment and sealed the deal.

This is what the Holy Spirit does: seals us for Jesus and guarantees our future with him.

After Jesus's troubling announcement of his departure, he gave his disciples a promise: It was actually *better* for them that he went away, because then he would send the Helper to them (John 16:7). Who is the Helper? "The Holy Spirit, whom the Father will send in my name," Jesus said, the Spirit of truth who reminds us of all God's promises (14:26). "He will glorify me," Jesus explained, "for he will take what is mine and declare it to you" (16:14).

Jesus, as a human, could be in only one place at a time.

But his Spirit would be present in *all* his people *all* the time.

This is why it was better for Jesus to leave—and now all his people benefit from this incredible promise, including us if we have trusted in him. *He sends his Holy Spirit to seal us as his own and guarantee our future.* He has our names written in heaven, and the Spirit is the down payment. Jesus has officially signed, sealed, and delivered the eternal security of his people. We belong to him, and his Spirit is living proof.

God's active presence with us through his Spirit means his tender care continues, but now it reverberates through the whole church, around the whole world. In this land in-between, as we long for everything to be made right, he has given us his Spirit so we won't lose heart. As you wait, how is Jesus with you, right now, through his Holy Spirit? What promises has he made to you?

The Promise of Glory in Weakness

Your body is a tent, a temporary dwelling place, ropes, pegs, and all (2 Corinthians 5:1–2). We are dust, and to dust we will return—yet the dust isn't the end. In John 17 Jesus prayed, "Father, I desire that they also, whom you have given me, may be with me where I am, *to see my glory* that you have given me because you loved me before the foundation of the world" (verse 24). Jesus wants all his people safely gathered into his resurrected, glorified presence—and what Jesus wants, Jesus gets. His blood seals the deal, his Spirit guarantees it, so we wait with patience.

Even now, our weakness reminds us that we are not our own, that we depend wholly on our Creator and Savior. Even the most difficult and frustrating of moments are opportunities to revel in God's glorious strength. Believe me, I can't wait to have a brand-new, strong body with no physical ailments or pains, but even better than this, one day I will see my Savior, whose very presence makes me new—body *and* soul. Until then, if our highest good is to be near Jesus and if weakness is what it takes to draw near to him, then we can lean into our weakness rather than despising it. Our weakness may be all we know right now, but soon we'll know nothing of it. Soon Jesus's glory will transform our earthly bodies to be like his own: "Now, our bodies are like Adam's body. But in heaven, our bodies will be like the body of Christ" (1 Corinthians 15:49, NLV). Weakness will give way to power, and dishonor to glory—a glory we share with Jesus because Jesus first gave up his glory to share in our weakness.

His Promise: God's Spirit will use your weakness to draw you nearer to his glory.

The Promise of Holiness in Temptation

In John 17 Jesus also prayed that all his disciples would be protected from Satan and his schemes: "I do not ask that you take them out of the world, but that you keep them from the evil one. . . . Sanctify them in the truth; your word is truth" (verses 15, 17). The word *sanctify* means "to make holy." How does Jesus guard us from evil and create in us a beauty that matches his? He prays for us, and his Spirit does too (Romans 8:26–27). He uses the protective sword of Scripture to help us wage war as we flee temptation, repent when we don't, turn anew to Jesus, and walk in obedience to his ways (Ephesians 6:17). "Holy living trains Christians for heaven," J. C. Ryle says. "The nearer we live to God while we live, the more ready we will be to dwell forever in his presence when we die."[1] On that day, we will no longer have the capacity to sin; we will finally be holy as he is holy, and fear and shame will be no more.[2] And until that day, we fight with all the strength he supplies and rest in his enduring grace when we fail.

His Promise: God's Spirit will help you fight sin, flee temptation, and rest in his grace.

The Promise of Love in Loneliness

"Lord, we do not know where you are going," Thomas said when Jesus announced he was leaving (John 14:5). But Jesus reassured his uncertain disciples, "I will not leave you as orphans; I will come to you. . . . If anyone loves me, he will keep my word, and my Father will love him, and we will come to him and make our home with him" (verses 18, 23). In other words, *you will never ever be truly alone.* To all those who are sealed by Jesus, he gives the down payment of his Spirit; then he takes up residence with us: "He dwells with you and will be in you" (verse 17). *We* become his Spirit's home, even as we wait for our heavenly home with him (verses 2–3). This means that Jesus, by the presence of his Spirit, is closer than your next breath. It means that you have fellowship with the living God and his constant, comforting friendship. It means that he will never leave or forsake you, even when everyone else does. And it means that someday loneliness will be a faint memory as we bask in the enjoyment of perfect, restored relationships, with Jesus and with one another.

His Promise: God's Spirit makes your heart his home and will never ever abandon you.

The Promise of Fruitfulness in Pain

Once the Spirit of Christ dwells in us, he doesn't leave us the same. Through his sometimes-painful pruning work, he makes us look more like Jesus: "I am the true vine, and my Father is the vinedresser. Every branch in me that does not bear fruit he takes away, and every branch that does bear fruit he prunes, that it may bear more fruit" (John 15:1–2). Lopping off fruitless branches and cutting back weak ones—those processes hurt. But they are not without purpose: God uses painful pruning to make us more fruitful.

What does his Spirit produce in us? The very heart of Jesus: "Love, joy, peace, patience, kindness, goodness, faithfulness, gentleness, self-control" (Galatians 5:22–23). So, when your pain persists with no end in sight, God's Spirit assures you he won't waste a thing. Instead, as you draw near to him in your pain, he infuses you with his very life: "Whoever abides in me and I in him, he it is that bears much fruit, for apart from me you can do nothing" (John 15:5).

The Spirit's promise also includes the total removal of every bodily affliction; nothing that plagues us now in our earthly tents will continue on into eternity: "What is mortal [will] be swallowed up by life" (2 Corinthians 5:4).

His Promise: God's Spirit will produce good fruit through pain, making you more like Jesus.

The Promise of Assurance in Doubt

We've already seen how doubt can plague anyone, even those who walked most closely with Jesus. But Jesus knew that persecution and many other pressures would threaten their faith, so he reassured them: "When the Spirit of truth comes, he will guide you into all the truth, for he will not speak on his own authority, but whatever he hears he will speak, and he will declare to you the things that are to come" (John 16:13). The Bible we know is the fulfillment of this promise, as Jesus guided his followers, by the Spirit, to pen the words of the New Testament.

If Jesus was that committed to preserving his truth, won't he do the same within us? Won't he see to it that his message will prevail? The Spirit of truth continues his ministry of assurance to every believer, leading us deeper into the riches of Christ. The question for us is, *Will we continue to seek the treasure and mine for truth in Scripture,* even and especially when we doubt?

Our doubts are temporary. On the day when Christ returns, our faith will become sight and we will melt with relief along with all those who have waited for him:

> It will be said on that day,
> "Behold, this is our God; we have waited for him, that
> he might save us.
> This is the LORD; we have waited for him;
> let us be glad and rejoice in his salvation."
> (Isaiah 25:9)

His Promise: God's Spirit will help you fight doubt as he deepens your faith in his Word of truth.

The Promise of Hope in Grief

Jesus was refreshingly honest with his disciples; he knew the grief they were about to experience: "You will be sorrowful, but your sorrow will turn into joy" (John 16:20). His awful crucifixion would break their hearts and dissolve their hopes. But that wouldn't be the end of the story. The dead would be raised, the grave would be emptied, and one man's resurrection would mark the beginning of a new era: "Just as Christ was raised from the dead by the glory of the Father, [so] we too might walk in newness of life" (Romans 6:4).

Why did Jesus choose to become a human? So we could become like him—sinless, faultless, and restored to the mirror image of God. Remember, Adam's sin devastated our humanity, but the sinlessness of Jesus would heal us. Our hope when we are grieving—whether loss and death or the many other sorrows of this in-between world—is the risen Jesus, *who lives*. Death's touch is temporary. One day, in the twinkling of an eye, Jesus will reappear and we will "move in" to our powerful, glorious, eternal bodies. The dead will be raised, and all the grief that death has caused will be buried forever: "The last enemy to be destroyed is death" (1 Corinthians 15:26). Our sadness will dissolve into a fullness of joy we can't begin to imagine. And "we will always be with the Lord" (1 Thessalonians 4:17).

His Promise: God's Spirit will restore you fully into his image, and everlasting joy will be yours.

FULLY KNOWN, FULLY LOVED

Do you yearn to be known and loved in the deepest parts of your soul? Do you long for the struggles of this in-between world to cease? You are not left without hope. For there is a place where our yearning souls find rest and our longing hearts are quenched in life-giving streams of peace—even as we wait for full redemption.

His name is Jesus. And he knows you by name.

As you come to the final pages of this book, our hope is that you know, beyond a doubt, that Jesus is wholeheartedly *for you*. He loved us enough to take on himself the very things we long to be freed from—the limitations, struggles, and full extent of our humanity.

But even more, he endured our humanity to overcome it, and he overcame it to redeem it—in part now but one day in full. Let the incredible implications of this sink in: You, dear reader, have hope in and beyond the bounds of your humanity because Jesus has been there—and now he offers you everything you need in himself if you will put your trust in him:

> As high as the heavens are above the earth,
> so great is his faithful love
> toward those who fear him.
> As far as the east is from the west,
> so far has he removed
> our transgressions from us.
> As a father has compassion on his children,
> so the LORD has compassion on those who fear him.
> For he knows what we are made of,
> remembering that we are dust. (Psalm 103:11–14, CSB)

In your weakness, he will meet you with his strength.
In your temptations, he will meet you with his power.
In your loneliness, he will meet you with his presence.
In your pain, he will meet you with his comfort.
In your doubt, he will meet you with his truth.
In your grief, he will meet you with his hope.
In your greatest joys and your deepest lows, he is there.

Though you must endure this in-between world a little while longer, the day will come when your sorrows will turn to joy, your mourning will turn to dancing, and all that is broken will finally be made whole.

But until that day comes, you can be assured of this: Jesus understands—and he will meet you there.

Meeting with Jesus

1. Write out Isaiah 26:3 and memorize it to remind yourself of the truths you've learned: "You will keep the mind that is dependent on you in perfect peace, for it is trusting in you" (CSB).
2. What might it look like to depend on God's promised helper, his Holy Spirit, even this week? How does Scripture help us do this?
3. Which of these promises most encourages you as you finish this book, and why? Write out five takeaways from the book that encouraged you or five areas you'd like God to help you grow in.

Epilogue

Jesus Will Meet You There

Come near to God and he will come near to you.
—James 4:8, NIV

As we bring this book to a close, we pray you have seen how Jesus isn't a far-off God but draws near to you in all aspects of your humanity. Even more, we hope you see how he is *for you,* breathing hope, forgiveness, purpose, strength, and redemption into the hearts of those who turn to him in faith.

But we'd be remiss if you walked away from this book encouraged but still wondering, *What now?*

What does it look like once you have come to Jesus for salvation but you're wondering how to grow and experience the nearness he promises? How are we supposed to respond to Jesus drawing near to us?

Although this isn't an exhaustive list, we encourage you to consider four practical steps toward growing in relationship with him.

READ HIS WORDS

The Bible is sixty-six books full of God's words written to us so we will know his character and promises and have the wisdom, comfort, encouragement, conviction, guidance, and hope we need for all of life. Second Timothy 3:16 tells us, "All Scripture is breathed out by God and profitable for teaching, for reproof, for correction, and for training in righteousness."

To paraphrase Charles Spurgeon, "Visit many books, but live in the Bible."[1] We can learn from the wisdom of others in many ways, but if we want to be drawn into the very presence of God, we have to fill our minds and hearts with the inspired words of God found in the Bible alone. Just as you grow in friendship by getting to know a person better (their character, personality, what makes them who they are), the more we get to know who God is, the closer we will grow in relationship with him.

As people who are still prone toward independence and the distractions of this world, there will be times when we don't *feel* like reading the Bible. That's why it's helpful to create a habit of reading his Word—even though it may look a little different in different seasons of life. Just as we discipline our bodies for the sake of our physical health, it's important for us to have spiritual disciplines for our spiritual health. We're motivated not by guilt and shame but by a desire to be near to the One who has promised to draw near to us. Satan may throw arrows of distraction and lies to keep you from coming to Jesus honestly in your need, but God always woos with a heart that longs to be near to his children.

You may be thinking, *But I don't know where to start.* Rest assured, you are *not* alone in that struggle. Like with most other things in life that feel daunting, it's helpful to start small. The goal is not to read an entire book of the Bible in one sitting but to read and dwell on a smaller portion that's more digestible. If you don't have much Bible knowledge, here are a few good places to start.

What to Read

1. Pick one of the Gospels (Matthew, Mark, Luke, or John) and read about the life of Jesus.

2. Read one psalm a day. Psalms is like a window into the humanity of some of the most faithful Christians of old, including King David. Not only are psalms relatable, but they also help us see the promises and character of God and apply them to the questions, emotions, and ups and downs of life.
3. Start at the beginning. Open your Bible to Genesis 1 and read the creation story in small portions to see the launching point of God's redemptive plan for humanity.

Most importantly, after you've read a portion of Scripture, we encourage you to ask some questions about what you've read—maybe even journaling your answers.

What to Ask

1. What does this tell me about who God is (his power, holiness, justice, etc.)?
2. What does this tell me about myself, and how might I apply the truth that I am reading? Do I see this struggle/sin/fear in my own heart? Is there a pattern of disobedience that I need to ask forgiveness for? Is there a truth that I need help believing? Is there a hurt that I need to apply God's words of comfort to? Is there unbelief in me that is at the root of a certain thought or behavior pattern?
3. Is there anything in the text that I don't understand? (If so, you can easily find various interpretations and answers in several free Bible commentaries available online. Or ask a fellow Christian who seems trustworthy in their knowledge of the Bible.)
4. Is there a promise of God that I can find rest or encouragement in today?

Although Bible reading may seem daunting at first, Jesus will meet you with his presence and help you understand his words and apply them to your life.

TALK WITH HIM

Can you imagine being in a friendship, a marriage, or any other relationship but you barely talk to that person? It wouldn't really be a relationship at all. You might know about them to some degree, but without engaging with them on a consistent personal level, you will never truly know them in an intimate way. The same is true with growing nearer to Jesus. If we don't listen to his words in Scripture and don't share our hearts with him in response, it will always remain a distant, stale relationship—if there's even a genuine relationship at all. But God doesn't want only our acknowledgment of him; he wants all of us. He longs for us to bring our fears and worries, our hopes and excitements, our griefs and sorrows, our guilt over the wrongs we've done, and all we need to him in prayer (simply conversing with him). We should always be willing to hear what he has to say to us through his Word and the Holy Spirit's leading, but he also wants to hear our hearts in response. *That* is the mark of a true, deepening relationship.

However, if prayer has been hard for you, know that you are in good company. At first, talking to the Lord can feel unnatural to us sensory beings. But the more we grow in our communication with him, the more we will also grow in an awareness of his presence and the gift of relationship with the living God. Our words don't have to be flowery or spiritually savvy; God simply wants to hear the honest cries of our hearts. But if you still struggle to find the words, a great place to start is to turn Scripture into your own personal prayers. Psalms can be a great launching point.

Here's a practical way of doing this with Psalm 31 as an example.

When you are overwhelmed or afraid:

In you, O Lord, do I take refuge;
let me never be put to shame;
in your righteousness deliver me!
Incline your ear to me;
rescue me speedily!
Be a rock of refuge for me,
a strong fortress to save me!

For you are my rock and my fortress;
and for your name's sake you lead me and guide me;
you take me out of the net they have hidden for me,
for you are my refuge. (verses 1–4)

When you are weary or grieved:

Be gracious to me, O Lord, for I am in distress;
my eye is wasted from grief;
my soul and my body also.
For my life is spent with sorrow,
and my years with sighing;
my strength fails because of my iniquity,
and my bones waste away. (verses 9–10)

When you need to remember his promises:

But I trust in you, O Lord;
I say, "You are my God."
My times are in your hand;
rescue me from the hand of my enemies and from my persecutors!
Make your face shine on your servant;
save me in your steadfast love! . . .

> Oh, how abundant is your goodness,
> which you have stored up for those who fear you
> and worked for those who take refuge in you,
> in the sight of the children of mankind! (verses 14–16, 19)

Friend, although you may not always *feel* like reading the Bible or praying, the more you step out in faith and make it a way of life, the more your heart will be drawn closer to Jesus's heart, and the more you will desire a growing relationship with him. Not only will Jesus be drawing near to you, but you will also, in fact, experience the riches of a personal relationship with the God of the universe as you draw near to him in return.

SPEND TIME WITH THE FAMILY OF GOD

Thankfully, God doesn't ask us to walk this road alone. Not only does he give us his Holy Spirit to live in us; he also encourages us to regularly spend time with other Christians, both worshipping together in a local gospel-preaching church and investing in one another's lives. Jesus shows us all throughout the Gospels that we were never meant to be an island. Jesus didn't spend most of his time on earth teaching in a synagogue. Most of his ministry came through doing life with those around him—eating around a table, fishing out on the lake, and drawing near to others in their pain and questions.

So what trusted friend or mentor can you reach out to today for mutual encouragement to grow in Christ?

We all need to be encouraged and spurred on, just as we have the blessing of encouraging and spurring on others in their walks with Jesus in a world full of hardship and things pulling for our affections. It's a gift to have the family of God—a family that is to be marked by loving one another as Christ has loved us, even as we do so imperfectly.

> Above all these put on love, which binds everything together in perfect harmony. And let the peace of Christ rule in your hearts, to which indeed you were called in one body. And be thankful. Let the word of Christ dwell in you richly, teaching and admonishing one another in all wisdom, singing psalms and hymns and spiritual songs, with thankfulness in your hearts to God. (Colossians 3:14–16)

The family of God is far from perfect, but it's still a gift. We encourage you to seek out a local church if you don't have one and, if possible, ask about groups that meet during the week. Being in a small group of other Christians enables you to be a support and encouragement to one another, learn God's Word together, and walk together as God intends.

As we draw near to God, the natural overflow will be to draw near to one another in the body of Christ. And what a blessing it can be.

ENJOY HIM

Last, remember that God is the God of all that is good, beautiful, and life-giving. Although this passing life is a jumbled mix of good and hard, God has given us so much to delight in and enjoy as reflections of his glory.

From sunrises and sunsets to rolling thunder and crashing waves, from the miraculous birth of a fawn to the impressive flight of a hummingbird, from the creativity of an artist to the brilliance of a precious diamond, from the warmth of coffee on a cold day to the wafting aroma of fresh-baked cookies, from the intuitive nuzzle of man's best friend to the endorphin shot of a belly laugh—all are good gifts to enjoy as they lead us to thankfulness for the Giver of those gifts.

Sometimes we can forget that the very nature of God is one of joy. Yes, *sometimes* the greatest joy he has for us must come through temporary hardships, but Jesus shines his smiling face on us in countless ways throughout each day. We just need eyes to see it and hearts willing to receive it.

Today take the time to stop and smell the roses. Call a friend and enjoy the gift of that friendship. Take a walk and soak up the sights and sounds that reflect the creativity and beauty of our Creator. Enjoy that hobby or talent. And when you do, thank the Lord for his good gifts to you, even amid the difficulties. You just might be surprised how much Jesus is all around you—drawing you into the joy of his presence.

Above all else, know that the Christian life is one long process of growth—and sometimes a painfully slow one. But as you learn to draw near to the God who has first drawn near to you, he will not leave you as you are. He will grow you ever so patiently, change you to be more like him, and lavish you with the immeasurable blessings of being in relationship with him.

In every moment in this wonderful, difficult land in between and in every complex part of your humanity, you can be assured of this: Jesus will meet you there.

Acknowledgments

KRISTEN

A writer feels the weight of every book written under the authority of God's precious Word—and this one was no exception. I'm so grateful to all those who have prayed, listened, read, and given us sharpening feedback. This book is stronger because of a company of invested and thoughtful people!

Brad, you're my best theological mind, my most devoted prayer, my strongest support, my dearest friend. Thank you for always believing in me and spurring me on when I've wanted to give up. And thanks for reminding me of the joy and privilege of being a writer.

To my three kids: You have so graciously loved me through writing seasons. (Joanna, thanks for your sweet "keep going!" note.) When my mind was often somewhere else, you three brought me back to earth. Being your mom is my favorite job! I pray that you will know the nearness of Jesus all your days and rest in his care for you.

Sarah, you are an answer to my prayers! How God brought us back together for this project amazes me, and I am so thankful for your friendship and writing gift. I keep telling people you have been "the wind beneath my wings" in this creative season.

Will, you took our book to heart, advocated for us, and made it much stronger. You have incredible editing and writing gifts, and I've learned much from you.

Don, thank you for representing us so well in a way that glorifies the Lord.

To Aaron, Elisa, Eric, Rachel, Linda: Thank you for taking the time to read, reread, and comment on our manuscript. Your insights have been invaluable!

And to Jesus, my Lord and Savior: All glory goes to you.

SARAH

All praise and honor to Jesus Christ, who has not only opened my eyes to the truth of the Gospel and given me life in his name, but has been a personal, near, and faithful Friend. Every word of this book is a testimony to his all-sufficient grace.

Thank you to my husband, Jeff, for your continual support and encouragement. You have patiently endured with me in moments when I was physically present but mentally living in the pages of this book as it was being written. You have encouraged me in my weariness, spurred me on in my doubts and insecurities, and loved me well through the relentless challenges of our life. Your steady and faithful presence is a gift. I wouldn't want to walk this road with anyone but you.

To my children, thank you for bearing with me through the endless ups and downs of this life. You have had a front-row seat to my weaknesses, failings, and hardships, but you have been amazing examples to me of God's grace through it all. I pray that you will all come to know the life-changing presence of Jesus in a profound and personal way. I thank God for each one of you.

To my pastors at Cross and Crown, thank you for not only faithfully teaching the Word, but also for being humble, wonderful men of God. I thank God for your integrity to the truth, your generous support for our family over the years, and your friendship.

Lastly, to our editor, Will, thank you for championing the heart of this message and helping Kristen and me shape, mold, and form this book into what it is. We thank God for the vision and gifts he's given you, to not only see the value of the message but also push and challenge us in a way that would ultimately bring the best out of us and our writing. You are truly a gifted editor and visionary!

Notes

2: When It's Hard to Be Human

1. Scripture tells us the creation groans with eager longing to be made new (Romans 8:19–22), and in that way the new creation will live forever. Will there be dogs in heaven? Maybe. But only human beings have eternal souls now that will continue to live forever then.
2. "Yet without sin," as the author of Hebrews tells us (4:15). This is ultimately what sets Jesus apart from every other human being; he alone was, and is, without sin.

3: When Nothing Seems to Calm Your Anxious Thoughts

1. *Oxford English Dictionary*, "anxiety," last updated September 2025, https://doi.org/10.1093/OED/5933092475.
2. Kelly M. Kapic, *You're Only Human: How Your Limits Reflect God's Design and Why That's Good News* (Brazos, 2022), 132.

5: When You Feel Like You Don't Measure Up

1. "The Bummer Lamb," Embracing Brokenness Ministries, accessed October 31, 2025, https://embracingbrokenness.org/2019/12/the-bummer-lamb.
2. "The Bummer Lamb."

6: When Change Feels Impossible

1. Mark Jones, *Knowing Christ* (Banner of Truth, 2015), 114.

7: When You Want to Hide

1. As we've mentioned, women in Jesus's time were considered inferior to men, with low social status.

2. J. C. Ryle, *St. John*, vol. 1, Expository Thoughts on the Gospels (Robert Carter & Brothers, 1879), 192.
3. Ryle, *St. John*, 217–18.

8: When Fear Consumes You

1. Vaneetha Rendall Risner, *Watching for the Morning: 90 Devotionals for When Hope Is Hard to Find* (B&H, 2025), chap. 7.

9: When You Wonder What God *Really* Thinks of You

1. I'm indebted to Dane Ortlund for pointing this out in his excellent book *Gentle and Lowly*. Dane Ortlund, *Gentle and Lowly: The Heart of Christ for Sinners and Sufferers* (Crossway, 2020).
2. Lexical Summary and Topical Lexicon, "4762. *strephó*," Bible Hub, https://biblehub.com/greek/4762.htm.
3. Ortlund, *Gentle and Lowly*, 71.
4. See chapter 6 for more about how we can change.
5. Robert Robinson, "Come, Thou Fount of Every Blessing," Hymnary.org, accessed November 18, 2025, https://hymnary.org/text/come_thou_fount_of_every_blessing.

10: When You Need a Friend

1. Jesus's human experience included the many joys of fellowship with other humans, along with his perfect relationship with the Father and Spirit. But he knew loneliness too.
2. *Strong's Exhaustive Concordance*, "3101. *mathéthés*," Bible Hub, https://biblehub.com/greek/3101.htm.
3. I am thankful to Jared Wilson for his wonderful book *Friendship with the Friend of Sinners: The Remarkable Possibility of Closeness with Christ* (Baker, 2023), where I learned much about how Jesus is my friend. I highly recommend it to you!

12: When You Worry That You're Not a Real Christian

1. Colin S. Smith, *Heaven, How I Got Here: The Story of the Thief on the Cross* (Christian Focus, 2015), 59.
2. Joni Eareckson Tada and Steven Estes, *When God Weeps: Why Our Sufferings Matter to the Almighty* (Zondervan, 1997), 53.
3. Remember, Jesus never sinned by thought or practice. Scripture is clear that he was without sin in himself. Yet, mystery of mysteries, he chose to bear our sin, *taking* it on himself.

4. George Bennard, "The Old Rugged Cross," Timeless Truths, accessed November 6, 2025, https://library.timelesstruths.org/music/The_Old_Rugged_Cross.
5. Donald S. Whitney, *Ten Questions to Diagnose Your Spiritual Health* (NavPress, 2021), 11.
6. Whitney, *Ten Questions,* 10.
7. Whitney, *Ten Questions,* 10.

13: When You Want to Be Healed

1. R. C. Sproul, "Accepting 'No' as God's Will," Ligonier, May 21, 2021, https://learn.ligonier.org/articles/accepting-no-gods-will.
2. Margaret Clarkson, *Grace Grows Best in Winter: Help for Those Who Must Suffer* (Eerdmans, 1984), 33.
3. Joni Eareckson Tada and Steven Estes, *When God Weeps: Why Our Sufferings Matter to the Almighty* (Zondervan, 1997), 84.

15: When You're Desperate for Change

1. Adapted from Kristen Wetherell, "Does Jesus Want to Heal Me?," The Gospel Coalition, March 13, 2017, www.thegospelcoalition.org/article/does-jesus-want-to-heal-me.
2. Bobby Jamieson, *Everything Is Never Enough: Ecclesiastes' Surprising Path to Resilient Happiness* (WaterBrook, 2025), 8, emphasis added.
3. Augustine, quoted in C. S. Lewis, *The Problem of Pain* (HarperOne, 2001), 94.

16: When the Miracle Doesn't Come

1. Corrie ten Boom, *The Hiding Place* (Chosen, 2006), 227.

17: When You Wonder If God's Punishing You

1. Paul David Tripp, *Everyday Gospel: A Daily Devotional Connecting Scripture to All of Life* (Crossway, 2024), 270.
2. Tripp, *Everyday Gospel,* 270–71.
3. C. H. Spurgeon, *Beside Still Waters: Words of Comfort for the Soul,* ed. Roy H. Clarke (Thomas Nelson, 1999), 116.

19: When You Fear Your Faith Will Fail

1. Joni Eareckson Tada, "The Stakes Are Higher Than You Think," Revive Our Hearts, September 24, 2010, www.reviveourhearts.com/events/true-woman-10-indianapolis/session/stakes-are-higher-you-think.

2. J. C. Ryle, *St. Luke*, vol. 2, Expository Thoughts on the Gospels (Robert Carter & Brothers, 1879), 410.
3. John Piper, "The Sifting of Simon Peter," Desiring God, April 26, 1981, www.desiringgod.org/messages/the-sifting-of-simon-peter.
4. Charles H. Spurgeon, *Morning by Morning: A New Edition of the Classic Devotional Based on The Holy Bible, English Standard Version*, ed. Alistair Begg (Crossway, 2007), 192.

21: When You Feel Alone in Your Doubts

1. Colin Smith, "Assurance Grows as We Listen to the Witness of the Spirit," The Orchard, December 8, 2024, https://theorchard.church/assurance-grows-as-we-listen-to-the-witness-of-the-spirit.
2. I recommend Ray Rhodes's books *Susie: The Life and Legacy of Susannah Spurgeon* (Moody, 2018) and *Yours, till Heaven: The Untold Love Story of Charles and Susie Spurgeon* (Moody, 2021).
3. You might start with some compilation books like *12 Faithful Women* (The Gospel Coalition, 2020), *Devoted* (Cruciform, 2018), or *5 Puritan Women* (Crossway, 2023), or dive deeper into specific individuals' stories.

22: When Death Seems to Win

1. One of the best treatments of this subject is B. B. Warfield's *The Emotional Life of Our Lord*, where he explores the range of emotions we see Jesus exhibit in Scripture.
2. As we've seen, Jesus is both fully God and fully man, divine and human, deity and flesh.
3. J. C. Ryle, *John*, vol. 2, Expository Thoughts on the Gospels, ed. Graham Hind and Mary Davis (Evangelical Press, 2024), 226.
4. After all, when Jesus was on earth, he was one person who could be in only one place at a time. Now he ministers to all his people through the presence of his Holy Spirit.
5. C. S. Lewis, *A Grief Observed* (HarperOne, 1994), 6.
6. "Whoever sings songs to a heavy heart is like one who takes off a garment on a cold day, and like vinegar on soda" (Proverbs 25:20).
7. Thayer's Greek Lexicon, "G1690. *embrimaomai*," Blue Letter Bible, www.blueletterbible.org/lexicon/g1690/kjv/tr/0-1.
8. Eric M. Schumacher, *Dads Hurt Too: A Father's Memoir of Miscarriage* (pub. by author, 2025), 51.
9. Matt Zoller Seitz, introduction to *The Wes Anderson Collection*, in *Bookends: Collected Intros and Outros*, ed. Michael Chabon (Harper Perennial, 2019), 3–4.
10. See Galatians 3:13–14 in *The Message* translation.

23: When Grief Dulls Your Senses

1. Joni Eareckson Tada, *A Place of Healing: Wrestling with the Mysteries of Suffering, Pain, and God's Sovereignty* (David C Cook, 2010), 61.
2. "Do the Next Thing," A Christian Home, accessed November 13, 2025, www.achristianhome.org/Good_Things/a_poem_quoted_by_elisabeth_elliot.htm.

25: When You Long for Jesus to Make It Right

1. J. C. Ryle, *John*, vol. 3, Expository Thoughts on the Gospels, ed. Graham Hind and Mary Davis (Evangelical Press, 2024), 162.
2. The fear of the Lord will still be present within us, for sure, but all earthly fears will finally fade in light of his presence with us.

Epilogue: Jesus Will Meet You There

1. C. H. Spurgeon, "Paul—His Cloak and His Books," sermon, Metropolitan Tabernacle, London, November 29, 1863, *Metropolitan Tabernacle Pulpit*, no. 542, 669, www.spurgeon.org/resource-library/sermons/paul-his-cloak-and-his-books/#flipbook/9.

About the Authors

Kristen Wetherell is a wife, mother, writer, and speaker. She is the author of numerous books, including *Hope When It Hurts, Help for the Hungry Soul*, and the For the Bible Tells Me So board book series. Kristen is a member of The Orchard and lives in Chicagoland with her husband and three children.

Sarah Walton is the co-author of the award-winning book *Hope When It Hurts; Together Through the Storms;* and *He Gives More Grace,* and the author of *Tears and Tossings* and *The Long Road Home*. She and her husband, Jeff, live in Colorado Springs with their four children.